Google Web Toolkit

GWT Java AJAX Programming

A practical guide to Google Web Toolkit for creating
AJAX applications with Java

Prabhakar Chaganti

BIRMINGHAM - MUMBAI

Google Web Toolkit

GWT Java Ajax Programming

First published: February 2007

Production Reference: 1150207

Published by Packt Publishing Ltd.
32 Lincoln Road
Olton
Birmingham, B27 6PA, UK.

ISBN 978-1-847191-00-7

www.packtpub.com

Cover Image by www.visionwt.com

Credits

Author

Prabhakar Chaganti

Reviewers

Luca Masini

Travis S. Schmidt

Development Editor

David Barnes

Assistant Development Editor

Nikhil Bangera

Technical Editors

Rashmi Phadnis

Ved Prakash Jha

Editorial Manager

Dipali Chittar

Project Manager

Patricia Weir

Project Coordinator

Suneet Amrute

Indexer

Bhushan Pangaonkar

Proofreader

Chris Smith

Layouts and Illustrations

Shantanu Zagade

Cover Designer

Shantanu Zagade

About the Author

Prabhakar Chaganti is an enterprise software architect and open-source evangelist working for a cutting-edge software company in the suburbs of Atlanta. His interests include Linux, Ruby, Python, Java, and Virtualization. He recently won the community choice award for the most innovative virtual appliance in the 2006 VMW—this award is the Ultimate Global Virtual Appliance Challenge.

This book has gained immense support from various people. The staff at Packt Publishing were very helpful in providing key assistance to me and ably and enthusiastically led me through the various phases of this project. I would like to thank the technical reviewers for their comments, which have helped make this a much better book. The vibrant community around the GWT mailing list was very helpful whenever I needed clarifications on some of the more arcane corners of GWT.

I would like to thank my wife Nitika for her support and constant encouragement while I was writing this book. She effortlessly played the roles of both mom and dad while I was wrestling with GWT! Thanks and love to my two daughters Anika and Anya for putting up with daddy being stuck to his laptop for long periods of time instead of playing with them.

About the Reviewers

Luca Masini was born in Florence in 1971. He is a senior software engineer and web architect. He has been heavily involved from the first days in the Java world as a consultant for the major Italian banks and firms, developing integration software, and as technical leader in many of the flagship projects. He worked for adoption of Sun's J2EE standard in an envinroment where COBOL was the leading language, and then he shifted his eyes toward open source, in particular IoC containers, ORM tools, and UI frameworks. As such he adopted early products like Spring, Hibernate, and Struts, giving customers a technlogical advantage. During last year he fell in love with GWT (of course !!) and he had to master a new project all done with Oracle's ADF Faces and JDeveloper as Visual IDE.

I want to thank my son Jacopo for being my lovely son and my wife for being the best wife a man can dream.

Travis S. Schmidt (BS, MBA) is currently employed as an Applications Developer at the University of Iowa Hygienic Laboratory. He has several years of experience in designing and developing web-based clients and recently deployed a system utilizing the Google Web Toolkit.

I would like to thank my loving family: Rebecca, Jacqueline, and Alexander, for the their unwavering support.

Table of Contents

Preface

The client-server architecture has undergone a vast change over a short period of time. Earlier, each application had a different client software, with the software serving as the UI. This software had to be installed individually on every client, and needed to be updated every time we made changes to the application. We moved from that to the web era and deploying applications on the Internet, and then Internet enabled us to use the omnipresent web browser for accessing our applications from anywhere. This was a sea change, but we still had issues of performance and applications not having the same feel or responsiveness as desktop applications. Enter AJAX, and now we can build web pages that can rival a desktop application in responsiveness and nifty looks. AJAX underpins the current trend in developing applications for the Internet known as Web 2.0. In order to build Ajaxified applications you need to know HTML, XML, and JavaScript at the very least.

The Google Web Toolkit (GWT) makes it even easier to design an AJAX application using just the Java programming language. It is an open-source Java development framework and its best feature is that we don't have to worry too much about incompatibilities between web browsers and platforms. In GWT, we write the code in Java and then GWT converts it into browser-compliant JavaScript and HTML. This helps a lot, because we can stop worrying about modular programming. It provides a programming framework that is similar to that used by developers building Java applications using one of the GUI toolkits such as Swing, AWT, or SWT. GWT provides all the common user-interface widgets, listeners to react to events happening in the widgets, and ways to combine them into more complex widgets to do things that the GWT team may never have envisioned! Moreover, it makes reusing chunks of program easy. This greatly reduces the number of different technologies that you will need to master. If you know Java, then you can use your favorite IDE (we use Eclipse in this book) to write and debug an AJAX GWT application in Java. Yes, that means you can actually put breakpoints in your code and debug seamlessly from the client side to the server side. You can deploy your applications in any servlet container, create and run unit tests, and essentially develop GWT applications like any Java application. So start reading this book, fire up Eclipse, and enter the wonderful world of AJAX and GWT programming!

In this book, we will start with downloading and installing GWT and walk through the creation, testing, debugging, and deployment of GWT applications. We will be creating a lot of highly interactive and fun user interfaces. We will also customize widgets and use JSNI to integrate GWT with other libraries such as Rico and Moo. fx. We will also learn to create our own custom widgets, and create a calendar and a weather widget. We will explore the I18N and XML support in GWT, create unit tests, and finally learn how to deploy GWT applications to a servlet container such as Tomcat. This book uses a typical task-based pattern, where we first show how to implement a task and then explain its working.

What This Book Covers

Chapter 1 introduces GWT, the download and installation of GWT, and running its sample application.

Chapter 2 deals with creation of a new GWT application from scratch, and using the Eclipse IDE with GWT projects, creating a new AJAX Random Quotes application, and running the new application.

Chapter 3 deals with an introduction to and overview of GWT asynchronous services, and creating a prime number service and a geocoder service.

Chapter 4 deals with using GWT to build simple interactive user interfaces. The samples included in this chapter are live search, auto fillable forms, sortable tables, dynamic lists, and a flickr-style editable label.

Chapter 5 introduces some of the more advanced features of GWT to build more complex user interfaces. The samples included in this chapter are pageable tables, editable tree nodes, a simple log spy, sticky notes, and a jigsaw puzzle.

Chapter 6 includes an introduction to JavaScript Native Interface (JSNI) and using it to wrap third-party Javascript libraries like Moo.fx and Rico. It also includes using the gwt-widgets project and its support for the Script.aculo.us effects.

Chapter 7 deals with creating custom GWT widgets. The samples included in this chapter are a calendar widget and a weather widget.

Chapter 8 concerns itself with creating and running unit tests for GWT services and applications.

Chapter 9 sees us using Internationalization (I18N) and client-side XML support in GWT.

Chapter 10 includes the deployment of GWT applications using both Ant and Eclipse.

What You Need for This Book

GWT needs Java SDK installed. It can be downloaded from the following site: `http://java.sun.com/javase/downloads/`. The safest version is to use with GWT is Java 1.4.2, as they are completely compatible with each other. Different versions of GWT are available for different operating systems, so you can use your favorite OS without any hassles.

Conventions

In this book, you will find a number of styles of text that distinguish between different kinds of information. Here are some examples of these styles, and an explanation of their meaning.

There are three styles for code. Code words in text are shown as follows: "The `GWT_HOME` directory contains a `samples` folder with seven applications."

A block of code will be set as follows:

```
public interface PrimesService extends RemoteService
{
  public boolean isPrimeNumber(int numberToVerify);
}
```

When we wish to draw your attention to a particular part of a code block, the relevant lines or items will be made bold:

```
calendarPanel.add(calendarGrid);
calendarPanel.add(todayButton);
```

Any command-line input and output is written as follows:

```
applicationCreator.cmd -out <directory location>\GWTBook\HelloGWT
                      com.packtpub.gwtbook.HelloGWT.client.HelloGWT
```

New terms and **important words** are introduced in a bold-type font. Words that you see on the screen, in menus or dialog boxes for example, appear in our text like this: "Click on the **Click me** button and you will get this window with your message."

 Warnings or important notes appear in a box like this.

Tips and tricks appear like this.

Reader Feedback

Feedback from our readers is always welcome. Let us know what you think about this book, what you liked or may have disliked. Reader feedback is important for us to develop titles that you really get the most out of.

To send us general feedback, simply drop an email to feedback@packtpub.com, making sure to mention the book title in the subject of your message.

If there is a book that you need and would like to see us publish, please send us a note in the **SUGGEST A TITLE** form on www.packtpub.com or email suggest@packtpub.com.

If there is a topic that you have expertise in and you are interested in either writing or contributing to a book, see our author guide on www.packtpub.com/authors.

Customer Support

Now that you are the proud owner of a Packt book, we have a number of things to help you to get the most from your purchase.

Downloading the Example Code for the Book

Visit http://www.packtpub.com/support, and select this book from the list of titles to download any example code or extra resources for this book. The files available for download will then be displayed.

The downloadable files contain instructions on how to use them.

Errata

Although we have taken every care to ensure the accuracy of our contents, mistakes do happen. If you find a mistake in one of our books—maybe a mistake in text or code—we would be grateful if you would report this to us. By doing this you can save other readers from frustration, and help to improve subsequent versions of this book. If you find any errata, report them by visiting http://www.packtpub.com/support, selecting your book, clicking on the **Submit Errata** link, and entering the details of your errata. Once your errata are verified, your submission will be accepted and the errata are added to the list of existing errata. The existing errata can be viewed by selecting your title from http://www.packtpub.com/support.

Questions

You can contact us at questions@packtpub.com if you are having a problem with some aspect of the book, and we will do our best to address it.

1
Getting Started

The **Google Web Toolkit (GWT)** is a revolutionary way to build **Asynchronous JavaScript and XML (AJAX)** applications that are comparable in responsiveness and look and feel to desktop applications.

In this chapter, we will look at:

- An introduction to GWT
- Downloading GWT
- Exploring the GWT samples
- The GWT License

Introduction to GWT

AJAX applications are great for creating web applications that are highly interactive and provide a great user experience, while being comparable to desktop applications in functionality, without the hassle of downloading or installing anything.

AJAX applications combine XML data interchange along with HTML and CSS for styling the interface, the XMLHttpRequest object for asynchronous communication with the server application, and JavaScript for dynamic interaction with the provided data. This enables one to build applications that are part of the Web 2.0 revolution—web applications that rival a desktop application in responsiveness. We can build web pages using AJAX to communicate with the server in the background, without reloading the page. We can even replace different sections of the displayed web page without refreshing the page. AJAX, finally enables us to take the traditional desktop-oriented applications, such as word processors, spreadsheets, and drawing programs, and serve them to users via the Web.

The GWT provides a Java-based development environment that enables you to build AJAX applications using the Java language. It encapsulates the XMLHttpRequest object API, and minimizes the cross-browser issues. So, you can quickly and efficiently build AJAX applications without worrying too much about tailoring your code to work in various browsers. It allows you to leverage the **Standard Widget Toolkit (SWT)** or Swing style programming by providing a framework that enables you to combine widgets into user interfaces. This is a great way to improve productivity and shorten your development time lines, by leveraging your knowledge of the Java programming language and your familiarity with the event-based interface development framework.

GWT provides a set of ready-to-use user interface widgets that you can immediately utilize to create new applications. It also provides a simple way to create innovative widgets by combining the existing ones. You can use the Eclipse IDE to create, debug, and unit-test your AJAX applications. You can build RPC services to provide certain functionalities that can be accessed asynchronously from your web applications easily using the GWT RPC framework. GWT enables you to integrate easily with servers written in other languages, so you can quickly enhance your applications to provide a much better user experience by utilizing the AJAX framework.

By the end of this book you will:

- Learn how GWT works
- Create effective AJAX applications quickly
- Create custom reusable widgets for your applications
- Create back-end RPC services that can be easily used from your AJAX applications

Basic Download

We are going to download GWT and its prerequisites, install them to the hard disk, and then run one of the sample applications shipped with the GWT distribution to ensure that it works correctly.

Time for Action—Downloading GWT

In order to use the GWT, you will need to have Java SDK installed. If you do not already have the Java SDK, you can download the latest version from http://java.sun.com/javase/downloads/. Install the SDK using the instructions provided by the download for your platform.

Java 1.4.2 is the safest version of Java to use with GWT, as it is completely compatible with this version, and you can be sure that your application code will compile correctly. GWT also works with the two newer versions of the Java platform—1.5 and 1.6; however, you will not be able to use any of the newer features of the Java language introduced in these versions in your GWT application code

Now, you are ready to download GWT:

1. GWT is available for Windows XP/2000, Linux, and Mac OS X platforms from the GWT download page (`http://code.google.com/webtoolkit/download.html`). This download includes the GWT compiler, hosted web browser, GWT class libraries, and several sample applications.

    Please read the Terms and Conditions of usage before downloading it. The latest version available is 1.3 RC 1, released December 12, 2006. Select the file for your platform. Here is a sample window showing the versions available for GWT:

    ### Version 1.3 RC 1

    As of version 1.3, Google Web Toolkit is licensed under the Apache 2.0 open source license, which includes limitations of liability and disclaimers of warranty for the product. Please note that some included libraries may be licensed under other open source licenses listed here.

    If you want to test our upcoming release, you can download Version 1.3 RC 1, released December 12, 2006 (release notes):

Platform	Package	Size	MD5 Sum
Windows XP/2000	gwt-windows-1.3.1.zip	13 MB	3cf7032d5001a7ae7a83555fcfc177cb
Mac OS X	gwt-mac-1.3.1.tar.gz	16 MB	92bb43d8967fff6b3140bb8433cf22f06
Linux (GTK+ 2.2.1+)	gwt-linux-1.3.1.tar.gz	22 MB	45515ce61756555d52e584ff36ea973a

2. Unzip the downloaded GWT distribution to your hard disk. It will create a directory named `gwt-windows-xxx` on Windows and `gwt-linux-xxx` on Linux, where xxx is the version number of the downloaded distribution. We will refer to the directory that contains the unzipped distribution as `GWT_HOME`. The `GWT_HOME` directory contains a `samples` folder with seven applications.

3. In order to ensure that the GWT is correctly installed, run the `Hello` sample application for your platform by executing the startup script for your platform (the executable scripts for Windows have the extension `.cmd` and the ones for Linux have the extension `.sh`).

    Execute the `Hello-shell` script for your platform. Here is a screenshot of the `Hello` application running successfully in the hosted GWT browser:

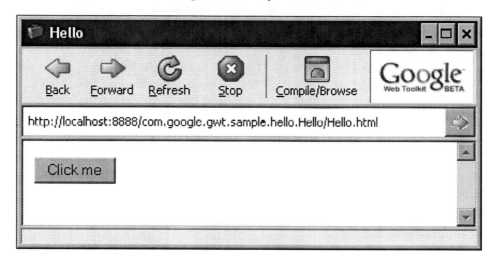

    Click on the **Click me** button and you will get a dialog box as follows:

What Just Happened?

The `GWT_HOME` directory contains all the scripts, files, and libraries needed for GWT development, which are as follows:

*   `doc`: This directory contains the API documentation for the various GWT classes. The API documentation is provided in two formats—the Google custom format and the familiar `javadoc` format.

*   `samples`: A directory that contains the sample applications.

- `gwt-*.jar`: These are the Java libraries that contain the GWT classes.
- `index.html`: This file is used as Readme for the GWT. It also provides a starting point for the GWT documentation along with pointers to other sources of information.
- `gwt-ll.dll` and `swt-win32-3235.dll`: These are Windows' shared libraries (Windows only).
- `libgwt-ll.so`, `libswt-gtk-3235.so`, `libswt-mozilla17-profile-gcc3-gtk-3235.so`, `libswt-mozilla17-profile-gtk-3235.so`, `libswt-mozilla-gcc3-gtk-3235.so`, `libswt-mozilla-gtk-3235.so`, and `libswt-pi-gtk-3235.so`: These are Linux shared libraries (Linux only).
- `applicationCreator`: This is a Script file for creating a new application.
- `junitCreator`: This is a Script file for creating a new JUnit test.
- `projectCreator`: This is a Script file for creating a new project.
- `i18nCreator`: This is a Script file for creating internationalization scripts.

When you executed `Hello-shell.cmd`, you started up the GWT development shell and provided the `Hello.html` file as a parameter to it. The development shell then launched a special hosted web browser and displayed the `Hello.html` file in it. The hosted web browser is an embedded SWT web browser that has hooks into the Java Virtual Machine (JVM). This makes it possible to debug the Java code for the application, using a Java development environment such as Eclipse.

Here is a screenshot of the development shell that starts up first:

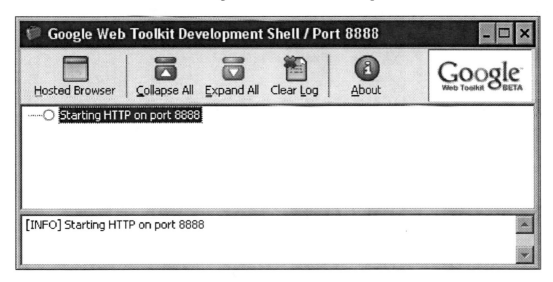

There's More!

You can customize several of the options provided to the GWT development shell on startup. Run the development shell, from a command prompt, in the GWT_HOME directory to see the various options available:

```
@java -cp "gwt-user.jar;gwt-dev-windows.jar" com.google.gwt.dev.
                                            GWTShell -help
```

You will see a screen similar to this one:

```
C:\gwt-windows-1.3.1>@java -cp "gwt-user.jar;gwt-dev-windows.jar" com.google.gwt.dev.GWTShell -help
Google Web Toolkit 1.3.1
GWTShell [-port port-number] [-noserver] [-whitelist whitelist-string] [-blacklist blacklist-string] [-log
-gen dir] [-out dir] [-style style] [url]

where
   -port       Runs an embedded Tomcat instance on the specified port (defaults to 8888)
   -noserver   Prevents the embedded Tomcat server from running, even if a port is specified
   -whitelist  Allows the user to browse URLS that match the specified regexes (comma or space separated)
   -blacklist  Prevents the user browsing URLS that match the specified regexes (comma or space separated)
   -logLevel   The level of logging detail: ERROR, WARN, INFO, TRACE, DEBUG, SPAM, or ALL
   -gen        The directory into which generated files will be written for review
   -out        The directory to write output files into (defaults to current)
   -style      Script output style: OBF[USCATED], PRETTY, or DETAILED (defaults to OBF)
and
   url         Automatically launches the specified URL
```

If you want to try out different settings, such as a different port numbers, you can modify the Hello-shell.cmd file to use these options.

The Linux version of GWT contains 32-bit SWT library bindings that are used by the hosted web browser. In order to run the samples or use the GWT hosted browser on a 64-bit platform such as AMD64, you need to do the following:

- Use a 32-bit JDK with 32-bit binary compatibility enabled.
- Set the environment variable LD_LIBRARY_PATH to the Mozilla directory in your GWT distribution, before starting the GWT shell.

Exploring the GWT Samples

Google provides a set of sample applications with the GWT distribution, which demonstrate several of its features. This task will explain how to run one of these samples—the KitchenSink application.

Time for Action—Getting into KitchenSink

There are seven sample applications provided with the GWT distribution—Hello, DynaTable, I18N, JSON, KitchenSink, SimpleXML, and Mail, each of which demonstrates a set of GWT features. In this task, we will explore the KitchenSink sample application, as it demonstrates all of the user-interface widgets that are provided with GWT. So, let's get into KitchenSink:

1. Run the KitchenSink application for your platform by executing the KitchenSink-shell script in the GWT_HOME/samples/KitchenSink directory. Here is the KitchenSink application:

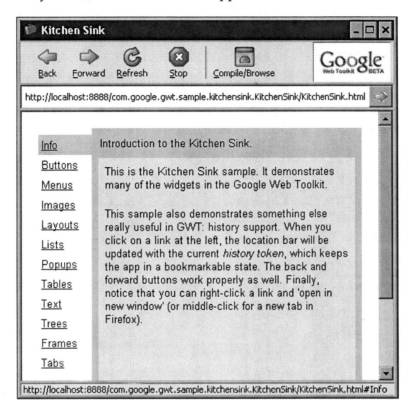

2. Click on the **Compile/Browse** button. The KitchenSink application will be automatically compiled and the system browser for your platform will start up and display the KitchenSink application.

3. Explore the application by clicking on each of the widget names in the navigation tree on the left. The frame on the right will display the selected widget and its variations. We will be using most of these widgets to build AJAX applications in later tasks.

4. You can add the KitchenSink sample as an Eclipse project to your workspace and browse the Java source code that is eventually compiled into HTML and JavaScript by the GWT compiler. We can use the projectCreator file helper script provided by GWT to generate the Eclipse project files for the KitchenSink application.

5. Navigate to your GWT_HOME directory and run the following command in a command prompt.

```
projectCreator.cmd -eclipse -ignore -out samples\KitchenSink
```

This will create the Eclipse platform project files, which can be imported into your Eclipse workspace. We will learn more about this script in the next chapter, when we create a new application from scratch.

6. Import the samples/KitchenSink/.project file into your Eclipse workspace. You can follow the above steps for each of the sample projects to generate their Eclipse project files, and then import them into your workspace. Here is an Eclipse workspace displaying the KitchenSink.java file:

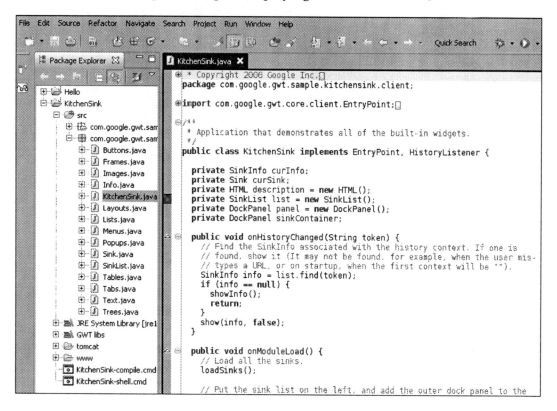

If you know how to program in Java, you can build an AJAX application using GWT, without any exposure to the complexities of either the XMLHttpRequest object API or the variations in the various browser implementations of the XMLHttpRequest object API.

What Just Happened?

The GWT development shell starts up, and runs the hosted web browser with the KitchenSink application running in it. The shell contains an embedded version of the Tomcat servlet container that listens on port 8888. When you run in the web mode, the application is compiled into HTML and JavaScript from Java. The compiled application is stored in the KitchenSink/www directory, and this directory itself is registered as a web application with Tomcat. This is how Tomcat is able to serve up the application to requesting web browsers.

As long as the development shell is running, you can even use other external web browsers to connect to the KitchenSink application by using the URL http://localhost:8888/com.google.gwt.sample.kitchensink.KitchenSink/ KitchenSink.html.

However, when we use an external browser to connect to the development shell, we cannot use breakpoints, and thus lose the debug capabilities provided when we run the application using the hosted browser. In order to access the application from another computer, ensure that you use either a DNS-resolvable machine name or the machine's IP address instead of localhost.

GWT consists of four main components that are layered together to provide the framework for writing AJAX applications using the toolkit:

- **GWT Java-to-JavaScript Compiler**: You use the GWT compiler to compile your GWT applications to JavaScript. The application can then be deployed to a web container. This is referred to as running in web mode. When you click on the **Compile/Browse** button, the Java code for the KitchenSink project is compiled by the Java-to-JavaScript compiler into pure HTML and JavaScript. The resulting artifacts are copied automatically to the KitchenSink/www folder.

- **GWT Hosted Web Browser**: This enables you to run and execute your GWT applications as Java in the Java Virtual Machine (JVM) without compiling to JavaScript first. This is referred to as running in hosted mode. GWT accomplishes this by embedding a special SWT browser control that contains hooks into the JVM. This special browser utilizes an Internet Explorer control on Windows or a Mozilla control on Linux. When you run the KitchenSink sample, the embedded SWT browser is what you see displaying the application.

- **JRE emulation library**: This contains JavaScript implementations of most of the widely used classes of the `java.lang` and `java.util` packages from the Java standard class library. Only some of the commonly used classes from these two packages are supported. None of the other Java packages in the JDK are currently part of this emulation library. These are the only classes that can be used by you for the client side of the AJAX application. You are of course free to use the entire Java class library for the server-side implementation. The Java code in the `KitchenSink` project is compiled into JavaScript using this emulation library.

- **GWT Web UI class library**: This provides a set of custom interfaces and classes that enable you to create various widgets such as buttons, text boxes, images, and text. GWT ships with most of the widgets commonly used in web applications. This is the class library that provides the Java widgets that are used in the `KitchenSink` application.

GWT License

Check if the GWT license is appropriate for you. These are the main features that you need to keep in mind:

- The GWT is open source and provided under an Apache Open Source License 2.0 — `http://www.apache.org/licenses/`.

- The third-party libraries and products that are bundled with the GWT distribution are provided under licensing detailed on this page — `http://code.google.com/webtoolkit/terms.html#licenses`.

- You can use GWT for building any kind of applications (commercial or non commercial).

- The application and the code for the application belong to the application's developer and Google does not have any rights to it.

You can use GWT to build any application you want and distribute the application under any license. You can also distribute the Java, HTML, JavaScript, and any other content generated by the GWT, along with the GWT tools that were used to generate that content, as long as you follow the terms of the Apache License.

Summary

In this chapter, we learned about the basic components of GWT. We saw how to download and install GWT, and explored the GWT sample application. Finally, we discussed the licensing terms for GWT.

In the next chapter, we will learn how to create a new GWT application from scratch.

2
Creating a New GWT Application

In this chapter, we will use the GWT tools to generate a skeleton project structure and files, with and without Eclipse support. We will then create our first AJAX application (a random quote application) by modifying the generated application to add functionality and finally run the application in both hosted and web mode.

The tasks that we will address are:

- Generating a new application
- Generating a new application with Eclipse support
- Creating a random quote AJAX application
- Running the application in hosted mode
- Running the application in web mode

Generating a New Application

We will generate a new GWT application by using one of the GWT scripts. These helper scripts provided by GWT create the skeleton of a GWT project with the basic folder structure and initial project files, so that we can get started in creating our new application as quickly as possible.

Time for Action—Using the ApplicationCreator

The GWT distribution contains a command-line script named `applicationCreator` that can be used to create a skeleton GWT project with all the necessary scaffolding. To create a new application, follow the steps given below:

1. Create a new directory named `GWTBook`. We will refer to this directory location as `GWT_EXAMPLES_DIR`. This folder will contain all the projects that will be created while performing the various tasks in this book.

2. Now create a subdirectory and name it `HelloGWT`. This directory will contain the code and the files for the new project that we are going to create in this chapter.

3. Run the `GWT_HOME\applicationCreator` by providing the following parameters in the command prompt:

```
applicationCreator.cmd -out <directory location>\GWTBook\HelloGWT
                       com.packtpub.gwtbook.HelloGWT.client.HelloGWT
```

The `-out` parameter specifies that all the artifacts be generated in the directory named `HelloGWT`. The fully qualified class name provided as the last parameter is used as the name of the class that is generated by the `applicationCreator` script and marked as the `EntryPoint` class for this application (we will cover the `EntryPoint` class in the next section).

The above step will create the folder structure and generate several files in the `GWT_EXAMPLES_DIR\HelloGWT` directory as shown in the following screenshot:

```
C:\gwt-windows-1.3.1>applicationCreator.cmd -out C:\GWTBook\HelloGWT com.packtpub.gwtbook.HelloGWT.client.HelloGWT
Created directory C:\GWTBook\HelloGWT\src
Created directory C:\GWTBook\HelloGWT\src\com\packtpub\gwtbook\HelloGWT
Created directory C:\GWTBook\HelloGWT\src\com\packtpub\gwtbook\HelloGWT\client
Created directory C:\GWTBook\HelloGWT\src\com\packtpub\gwtbook\HelloGWT\public
Created file C:\GWTBook\HelloGWT\src\com\packtpub\gwtbook\HelloGWT\HelloGWT.gwt.xml
Created file C:\GWTBook\HelloGWT\src\com\packtpub\gwtbook\HelloGWT\public\HelloGWT.html
Created file C:\GWTBook\HelloGWT\src\com\packtpub\gwtbook\HelloGWT\client\HelloGWT.java
Created file C:\GWTBook\HelloGWT\HelloGWT-shell.cmd
Created file C:\GWTBook\HelloGWT\HelloGWT-compile.cmd
```

What Just Happened?

The `applicationCreator` script invokes the `ApplicationCreator` class in `gwt-dev-xxx.jar`, which in turn creates the folder structure and generates the application files. This makes it very easy to get started on a new project as the whole structure for the project is automatically created for you. All you need to do is start filling in the application with your code to provide the desired functionality. A uniform way of creating projects also ensures adherence to a standard directory structure, which makes it easier for you when you are working on different GWT projects.

Here are all the files and folders that were automatically created under the
GWT_EXAMPLES_DIR\HelloGWT directory when we ran the applicationCreator
command:

- src
- HelloGWT-compile.cmd
- HelloGWT-shell.cmd

src: This folder contains all the generated source and configuration files for the
applications, contained in the familiar Java package structure, with the root package
being com.packtpub.gwtbook.hellogwt. This package name was deduced by
applicationCreator from the fully qualified class name that we provided as a
parameter to it. The generated files under this directory are:

- com\packtpub\gwtbook\hellogwt\HelloGWT.gwt.xml: This is the project
  module—an XML file that holds the entire configuration needed by a GWT
  project. The inherits tag specifies modules inherited by this module. In
  this simple case, we are inheriting only the functionality provided by the
  User module, which is built into the GWT. On more complex projects,
  module inheritance provides a nice way to reuse pieces of functionality.
  The EntryPoint refers to the class that will be instantiated by the GWT
  framework when the module is loaded. This is the class name provided
  to the applicationCreator command, when we created the project. The
  following code can be found in this file:

  ```
  <module>
  <!-- Inherit the core Web Toolkit stuff.-->
  <inherits name="com.google.gwt.user.User"/>
  <!-- Specify the app entry point class. -->
  <entry-point class=
              "com.packtpub.gwtbook.hellogwt.client.HelloGWT"/>
  </module>
  ```

- com\packtpub\gwtbook\hellogwt\client\HelloGWT.java: This is
  the entry point for our application. It extends the EntryPoint class, and
  when the HelloGWT module is loaded by the GWT framework, this class
  is instantiated and its onModuleLoad() method is automatically called. In
  this generated class, the onModuleLoad() method creates a button and a
  label, and then adds them to the page. It also adds a click listener for the
  button. We will be modifying the code in HellowGWT.java to create a new
  application later in this chapter. The current code in this file is as follows:

  ```
  package com.packtpub.gwtbook.hellogwt.client;
  import com.google.gwt.core.client.EntryPoint;
  import com.google.gwt.user.client.ui.Button;
  ```

```
import com.google.gwt.user.client.ui.ClickListener;
import com.google.gwt.user.client.ui.Label;
import com.google.gwt.user.client.ui.RootPanel;
import com.google.gwt.user.client.ui.Widget;
/** Entry point classes define <code>onModuleLoad()</code>. */
public class HelloGWT implements EntryPoint
{
  /** This is the entry point method. */
  public void onModuleLoad()
  {
    final Button button = new Button("Click me");
    final Label label = new Label();
    button.addClickListener(new ClickListener()
    {
      public void onClick(Widget sender)
      {
        if (label.getText().equals(""))
        label.setText("Hello World!");
        else
        label.setText("");
      }
    }
    //Assume that the host HTML has elements defined whose
    //IDs are "slot1", "slot2". In a real app, you probably
    //would not want to hard-code IDs. Instead, you could,
    //for example, search for all elements with a
    //particular CSS class and replace them with widgets.
    RootPanel.get("slot1").add(button);
    RootPanel.get("slot2").add(label);
  }
```

- com\packtpub\gwtbook\hellogwt\public\HelloGWT.html: This is a generated HTML page that loads the HelloGWT application and is referred to as the **host page**, as this is the web page that hosts the HelloGWT application. Even though this HTML file is deceptively simple, there are some points that you need to be aware of:

    ○ Firstly, it contains a meta tag that points to the HelloGWT module directory. This tag is the connection between the HTML page and the HelloGWT application. The following code represents this connection:

    ```
    <meta name='gwt:module'
          content='com.packtpub.gwtbook.hellogwt.HelloGWT'>
    ```

- Secondly, the `script` tag imports code from the `gwt.js` file. This file contains the code (shown below) required to bootstrap the GWT framework. It uses the configuration in the `HelloGWT.gwt.xml` file, and then dynamically loads the JavaScript created by compiling the `HelloGWT.java` file to present the application. The `gwt.js` file does not exist when we generate the skeleton project. It is generated by the GWT framework when we run the application in hosted mode or when we compile the application.

  ```
  <script language="JavaScript" src="gwt.js"></script>
  ```

- `HelloGWT-compile.cmd`: This file contains a command script for compiling the application into HTML and JavaScript.

- `HelloGWT-shell.cmd`: This file contains a command script for running the application in the hosted mode.

There is a well-defined relationship between these generated files. The `HelloGWT.html` file is the host page that loads the `gwt.js` file.

There's More!

The `applicationCreator` provides options to control several parameters for a new application. You can see these options by executing it from the following command line:

```
applicationCreator.cmd -help
```

```
C:\gwt-windows-1.3.1>applicationCreator.cmd -help
Google Web Toolkit 1.3.1
ApplicationCreator [-eclipse projectName] [-out dir] [-overwrite] [-ignore] className

where
    -eclipse    Creates a debug launch config for the named eclipse project
    -out        The directory to write output files into (defaults to current)
    -overwrite  Overwrite any existing files
    -ignore     Ignore any existing files; do not overwrite
and
    className   The fully-qualified name of the application class to create
```

`className` is the only required parameter for the `applicationCreator`. All the other parameters are optional. Here are some different ways to run `applicationCreator`:

- Create a new application without the Eclipse debug support:

  ```
  applicationCreator.cmd -out C:\GWTBook\Test1
                         com.packtpub.gwtbook.Test1.client.Test1
  ```

- Create a new application with the Eclipse debug support:

```
applicationCreator.cmd -eclipse -out C:\GWTBook\Test1
                    com.packtpub.gwtbook.Test1.client.Test1
```

- Create a new application with the Eclipse debug support that overwrites any previously generated classes with the same name:

```
applicationCreator.cmd -eclipse -overwrite -out C:\GWTBook\Test1
                    com.packtpub.gwtbook.Test1.client.Test1
```

Google recommends the following package naming convention for the source code for a GWT application. This will separate your project code by its functionality.

- `client`: This holds all the client-related application code. This code can only use the Java classes from the `java.util` and `java.lang` packages that are provided by the GWT's JRE Emulation library.

- `public`: This contains all the static web resources that are needed by the application, such as the HTML files, stylesheets, and image files. This directory includes the host page, which is the HTML file that contains the AJAX application (`HelloGWT.html` in the above case).

- `server`: This contains server-side code. These classes can use any Java class and any Java library to provide the functionality.

The modules for the application, such as `HelloGWT.gwt.xml` must be placed in the root package directory as a peer to the client, public, and server packages.

Generating a New Application with Eclipse Support

GWT comes out of the box with support for debugging GWT applications in the Eclipse IDE. This is a tremendously useful and time-saving feature. In this section, we are going to learn how to create new applications with the Eclipse IDE support.

Time for Action—Modifying HelloGWT

The `HelloGWT` application that we have created in the previous task works fine and we can make modifications to it, and run it easily. However, we are not taking advantage of one of GWT's biggest benefits — Eclipse IDE support that enhances the entire development experience. We will now recreate the same `HelloGWT` application, this time as an Eclipse project. It would have been nice if we could take the project that we created in the previous task and add Eclipse support for it. However, GWT does not support this at present. To do this, follow the steps given on the next page:

1. GWT provides a `projectCreator` script that creates Eclipse project files. Run the script with the parameters and you will see a screen as shown below:

   projectCreator.cmd -out E:\GWTBook\HelloGWT -eclipse HelloGWT

   ```
   C:\gwt-windows-1.3.1>projectCreator.cmd -out C:\GWTBook\HelloGWT -eclipse HelloGWT
   Created directory C:\GWTBook\HelloGWT\test
   Created file C:\GWTBook\HelloGWT\.project
   Created file C:\GWTBook\HelloGWT\.classpath
   ```

2. Now run the `applicationCreator` again with the parameters given below to create the HelloGWT project as an Eclipse project:

   applicationCreator.cmd -out E:\GWTBook\HelloGWT -eclipse HelloGWT
   **   -overwrite com.packtpub.gwtbook.hellogwt.client.HelloGWT**

   The `-overwrite` parameter will overwrite the files and folders in the `HelloGWT` directory. So, if you have made any changes that you would like to keep, please make sure you copy it to a different directory. You will see a screen as shown below:

   ```
   C:\gwt-windows-1.3.1>applicationCreator.cmd -out C:\GWTBook\HelloGWT -eclipse HelloGWT -overwrite com.packtpub.gwtbo
   elloGWT.client.HelloGWT
   Overwriting existing file C:\GWTBook\HelloGWT\src\com\packtpub\gwtbook\HelloGWT\HelloGWT.gwt.xml
   Overwriting existing file C:\GWTBook\HelloGWT\src\com\packtpub\gwtbook\HelloGWT\public\HelloGWT.html
   Overwriting existing file C:\GWTBook\HelloGWT\src\com\packtpub\gwtbook\HelloGWT\client\HelloGWT.java
   Overwriting existing file C:\GWTBook\HelloGWT\HelloGWT.launch
   Overwriting existing file C:\GWTBook\HelloGWT\HelloGWT-shell.cmd
   Overwriting existing file C:\GWTBook\HelloGWT\HelloGWT-compile.cmd
   ```

3. Import the newly created `HelloGWT` project into Eclipse. Navigate to the **Existing projects into Workspace** screen in Eclipse through the **File | Import** menu. Select the **HelloGWT** directory as the root folder, and click on the **Finish** button to import the project into your Eclipse workspace. Now you can edit, debug, and run your application, all from inside the Eclipse IDE!

4. Here are all the folders and files created after we have completed this task:

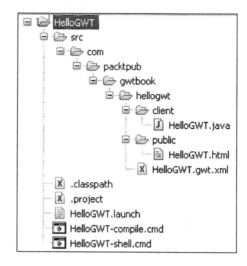

What Just Happened?

The projectCreator script invokes the ProjectCreator class in the gwt-dev-xxx.jar, which in turn creates the Eclipse project files. These files are then modified by applicationCreator to add the name of the project and classpath information for the project.

Here are the Eclipse-specific files created by running the projectCreator command:

- .classpath: Eclipse file for setting up the project classpath information

- .project: Eclipse project file with project name and builder information

- HelloGWT.launch: Eclipse configuration for launching the project from the **Run** and **Debug** Eclipse menus

There's More!

Here is a screenshot that displays the various options available for running the projectCreator when you run it from a command line with a -help option:

```
projectCreator.cmd -help
```

```
C:\gwt-windows-1.3.1>projectCreator.cmd -help
Google Web Toolkit 1.3.1
ProjectCreator [-ant projectName] [-eclipse projectName] [-out dir] [-overwrite] [-ignore]
where
  -ant        Generate an Ant buildfile to compile source (.ant.xml will be appended)
  -eclipse    Generate an eclipse project
  -out        The directory to write output files into (defaults to current)
  -overwrite  Overwrite any existing files
  -ignore     Ignore any existing files; do not overwrite
```

Creating a Random Quote AJAX Application

In this section, we will create our first AJAX application, which will display a random quote on the web page. This example application will familiarize us with the various pieces and modules in a GWT application, and lays the foundation for the rest of the book.

Time for Action—Modifying Auto-Generated Applications

We will create the above-mentioned application by modifying the auto-generated application from the previous task. The skeleton project structure that has been automatically created gives us a head start and demonstrates how quickly we can become productive using the GWT framework and tools.

The random quote is selected from a list of quotes stored on the server. Every second our application will retrieve the random quote provided by the server, and display it on the web page in true AJAX style — without refreshing the page.

1. Create a new Java file named `RandomQuoteService.java` in the `com.packtpub.gwtbook.hellogwt.client` package. Define a `RandomQuoteService` interface with one method to retrieve the quote:

    ```
    public interface RandomQuoteService extends RemoteService
    {
        public String getQuote();
    }
    ```

2. Create a new Java file named `RandomQuoteServiceAsync.java` in the `com.packtpub.gwtbook.hellogwt.client` package. Define a `RandomQuoteServiceAsync` interface:

    ```
    public interface RandomQuoteServiceAsync
    {
        public void getQuote(AsyncCallback callback);
    }
    ```

3. Create a new Java file named `RandomQuoteServiceImpl.java` in the `com.packtpub.gwtbook.hellogwt.server` package. Define a `RandomQuoteServiceImpl` class that extends `RemoteService` and implements the previously created `RandomQuoteService` interface. Add functionality to this class to return a random quote when the `getQuote()` method is called by a client.

```
public class RandomQuoteServiceImpl extends
           RemoteServiceServlet implements RandomQuoteService
{
  private Random randomizer = new Random();
  private static final long serialVersionUID=
                                        -1502084255979334403L;
  private static List quotes = new ArrayList();
  static
  {
    quotes.add("No great thing is created suddenly
                                        - Epictetus");
    quotes.add("Well done is better than well said
                                        - Ben Franklin");
    quotes.add("No wind favors he who has no destined port
                                        -Montaigne");
    quotes.add("Sometimes even to live is an act of courage
                                        - Seneca");
    quotes.add("Know thyself - Socrates");
  }
  public String getQuote()
           return (String) quotes.get(randomizer.nextInt(4));
  }
```

That's all we have to do for implementing functionality on the server. Now, we will modify the client to access the functionality we added to the server.

4. Modify `HelloGWT.java` to remove the existing label and button and add a label for displaying the retrieved quote. Add functionality in the `onModuleload()` to create a timer that goes off every second, and invokes the `RandomQuoteService` to retrieve a quote and display it in the label created in the previous step.

```
public void onModuleLoad()
{
  final Label quoteText = new Label();
  //create the service
  final RandomQuoteServiceAsync quoteService =
                            (RandomQuoteServiceAsync)GWT.create
                                (RandomQuoteService.class);
  //Specify the URL at which our service implementation is
  //running.
  ServiceDefTarget endpoint = (ServiceDefTarget)quoteService;
  endpoint.setServiceEntryPoint("/");
  Timer timer = new Timer()
  {
    public void run()
    {
```

```
//create an async callback to handle the result.
AsyncCallback callback = new AsyncCallback()
{
  public void onSuccess(Object result)
  {
    //display the retrieved quote in the label
    quoteText.setText((String) result);
  }
  public void onFailure(Throwable caught)
  {
    //display the error text if we cant get quote
    quoteText.setText("Failed to get a quote.");
  }
};
//Make the call.
quoteService.getQuote(callback);
  }
};
//Schedule the timer to run once every second
timer.scheduleRepeating(1000);
RootPanel.get().add(quoteText);
}
```

We now have the client application accessing the server to retrieve the quote.

5. Modify the HelloGWT.html to add a paragraph describing our AJAX application.

```
<p>
This is an AJAX application that retrieves a random quote from
the Random Quote service every second. The data is retrieved
and the quote updated without refreshing the page !
</p>
```

6. Let's make the label look nicer by adding a CSS for the label. Create a new file named HelloGWT.css in the com.packtpub.gwtbook.hellogwt.public package and add the following style class declaration to it:

```
quoteLabel
{
  color: white;
  display: block;
  width: 450px;
  padding: 2px 4px;
  text-decoration: none;
  text-align: center;
  font-family: Arial, Helvetica, sans-serif;
  font-weight: bold;
```

```
border: 1px solid;
border-color: black;
background-color: #704968;
text-decoration: none;
}
```

7. Modify the label to use this style in the `HelloGWT.java` file:

    ```
    quoteText.setStyleName("quoteLabel");
    ```

8. Add a reference to this stylesheet in the `HelloGWT.html` so the page can find the styles defined in the stylesheet.

    ```
    <link rel="stylesheet" href="HelloGWT.css">
    ```

9. The last thing we have to do is register our `RandomQuoteServiceImpl` servlet class in the `HelloGWT` module so that the client can find it. Add the following line to `HelloGWT.gwt.xml`:

    ```
    <servlet path="/" class="com.packtpub.gwtbook.hellogwt.server.
                            RandomQuoteServiceImpl"/>
    ```

    This servlet reference will be registered by the GWT framework with the embedded Tomcat servlet container, so that when you run it in the hosted mode, the context path `"/"` is mapped so that all requests to it are served by the `RandomQuoteServiceImpl` servlet.

Here are the folders and files in the `HelloGWT` project after completing all the above modifications:

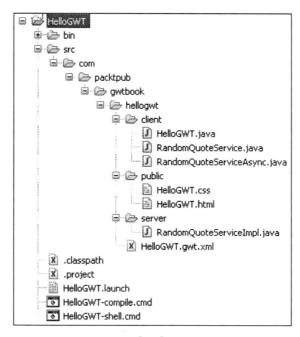

Our first AJAX application is now ready and we were able to create it entirely in Java without writing any HTML code!

What Just Happened?

The RandomQuoteService interface that we created is the client-side definition of our service. We also defined RandomQuoteServiceAsync, which is the client-side definition of the asynchronous version of our service. It provides a callback object that enables the asynchronous communication between the server and the client. The RandomQuoteServiceImpl is a servlet that implements this interface and provides the functionality for retrieving a random quote via RPC. We will look into creating services in detail in Chapter 3.

HelloGWT.java creates the user interface—just a label in this case—instantiates the RandomQuote service, and starts a timer that is scheduled to fire every second. Every time the timer fires, we communicate asynchronously with the RandomQuoteService to retrieve a quote, and update the label with the quote. The RootPanel is a GWT wrapper for the body of the HTML page. We attach our label to it so it can be displayed.

We modified the look and feel of the label by using a cascading stylesheet, and assigning the name of a style to the label in HelloGWT.java. We will learn more about using stylesheets and styles to beautify GWT in Chapter 6.

The user interface in this application is very simple. Hence we added the label straight to the RootPanel. However, in almost any non trivial user interface, we will need to position the widgets and lay them out more accurately. We can easily accomplish this by utilizing the various layout and panel classes in the GWT UI framework. We will learn how to use these classes in Chapters 4 and 5.

Running the Application in Hosted Mode

GWT provides a great way to test your application without deploying it but by running the application in a hosted mode. In this section, we will learn how to run the HelloGWT application in hosted mode.

Time for Action—Executing the HelloGWT-Shell Script

You can run the HelloGWT application in hosted mode by executing the HelloGWT-shell script. You can do this in three different ways:

- Executing the command script from the shell:

  Open a command prompt and navigate to the HelloGWT directory. Run HelloGWT-shell.cmd to start the HelloGWT application in hosted mode.

- Executing the command script from inside Eclipse:

  Double-click on the HelloGWT-shell.cmd file in the Eclipse **Package Explorer** or **navigator** view. This will execute the file and will start up the HelloGWT application in hosted mode.

- Running the HelloGWT.launcher from Eclipse:

  In Eclipse, navigate to the **Run** screen by clicking on the **Run | Run** link. Expand the **Java Application** node. Select the HelloGWT directory. Click on the **Run** link to launch the HelloGWT application in hosted mode.

You will see the following screen if the application runs properly:

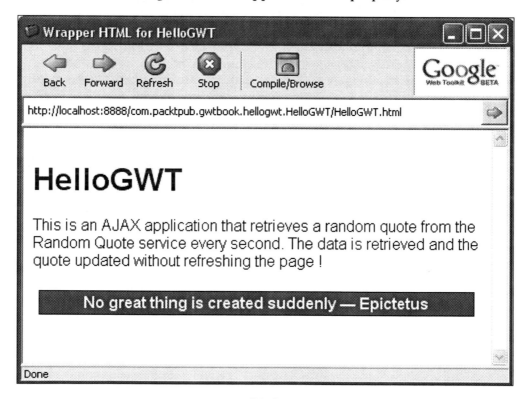

What Just Happened?

The command script executes the GWT development shell by providing it with the application class name as a parameter. The Eclipse launcher mimics the command script by creating a launch configuration that executes the GWT development shell from within the Eclipse environment. The launched GWT development shell loads the specified application in an embedded browser window, which displays the application. In hosted mode, the Java code in the project is not compiled into JavaScript. The application code is being run in the Java Virtual Machine as compiled bytecode.

Running the Application in Web Mode

In the previous section, we learned how to run GWT applications in hosted mode without deploying them. That is a great way to test and debug your application. However, when your application is running in a production environment, it will be deployed to a servlet container such as Tomcat. This task explains how to compile the HelloGWT application so that it can then be deployed to any servlet container. In GWT terms, this is referred to as running in the web mode.

Time for Action—Compile the Application

In order to run the HelloGWT application in web mode we need to do the following:

1. Compile the HelloGWT application first, by running the HelloGWT-compile script.

   HelloGWT-compile.cmd

2. The above step will create a www folder in the HelloGWT directory. Navigate to the www/com.packtpub.gwt.HelloGWT.HelloGWT directory.

3. Open the `HelloGWT.html` file in your web browser.

Everything needed to run the `HelloGWT` client application is contained in the www folder. You can deploy the contents of the folder to any servlet container and serve up the `HelloGWT` application. Here are the contents of the folder after completing the above steps:

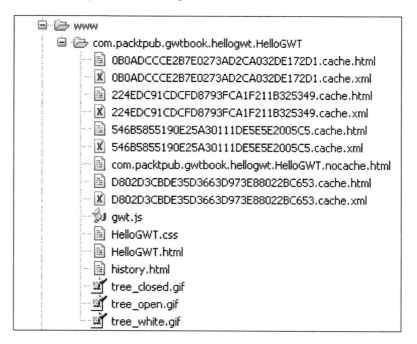

What Just Happened?

The `HelloGWT-compile` script invokes the GWT compiler and compiles all the Java source code in the `com.packtpub.gwt.hellogwt.client` package into HTML and JavaScript and copies it to the `www\com.packtpub.gwt.hellogwt.HelloGWT` directory. This directory name is automatically created by GWT, by removing the `client` portion from the fully qualified class name provided to `applicationCreator` previously. This folder contains a ready-to-deploy version of the `HelloGWT` client application. It contains:

- `HelloGWT.html`: The host page that functions as the main HTML page for the `HelloGWT` application.

- `gwt.js`: A generated JavaScript file that contains bootstrap code for loading and initializing the GWT framework.

- `History.html`: An HTML file that provides history management support.

- xxx-cache.html and xxx-cache.xml: One HTML and XML file per supported browser are generated. These contain the JavaScript code generated by the compilation of the source Java files in the com.packtpub. gwtbook.hellogwt.client and com.packtpub.gwtbook.hellogwt.server packages. For instance, in this case, on Windows, the compilation produced these files:

```
0B0ADCCCE2B7E0273AD2CA032DE172D1.cache.html
0B0ADCCCE2B7E0273AD2CA032DE172D1.cache.xml
224EDC91CDCFD8793FCA1F211B325349.cache.html
224EDC91CDCFD8793FCA1F211B325349.cache.xml
546B5855190E25A30111DE5E5E2005C5.cache.html
546B5855190E25A30111DE5E5E2005C5.cache.xml
D802D3CBDE35D3663D973E88022BC653.cache.html
D802D3CBDE35D3663D973E88022BC653.cache.xml
```

Each set of HTML and XML files represents one supported browser:

```
0B0ADCCCE2B7E0273AD2CA032DE172D1  - Safari
224EDC91CDCFD8793FCA1F211B325349  – Mozilla or Firefox
546B5855190E25A30111DE5E5E2005C5  – Internet Explorer
D802D3CBDE35D3663D973E88022BC653  - Opera
```

The file names are created by generating **Globally Unique Identifiers (GUIDs)** and using the GUID as part of the name. These file names will be different on different computers, and will also be different every time you do a clean recompile of the application on your computer. There is also a master HTML file generated (com.packtpub.gwtbook.hellogwt.HelloGWT. nocache.html) that selects the right HTML file from the above files and loads it, depending on the browser that is running the application.

The www folder does not contain the code from the com.packtpub.gwtbook. hellogwt.server package. This server code needs to be compiled and deployed in a servlet container so that the client application can communicate with the random quote service. We will learn about deploying to external servlet containers in Chapter 10. In normal development mode, we will use the hosted mode for testing, which runs the server code inside the embedded Tomcat servlet container in the GWT development shell. This makes it very easy to run and debug the server code from inside the same Eclipse environment as the client application code. This is another feature of GWT, which makes it an extremely productive environment for developing AJAX applications.

In the web mode, our client Java code has been compiled into JavaScript unlike in the hosted mode. Also, you will notice that the HelloGWT.gwt.xml is not in this directory. The configuration details from this module are included in the generated HTML and XML files above.

Thankfully, all this work is automatically done for us by the GWT framework when we run the HelloGWT-compile script. We can focus on the functionality provided by our AJAX applications and leave the browser-independent code generation and lower level XmlHttpRequest API to GWT.

We will learn how to deploy GWT applications to web servers and servlet containers in Chapter 10.

There's More!

You can also compile the HelloGWT application from the GWT development shell in hosted mode. Run the HelloGWT-shell command script to run the application in hosted mode. Click on the **Compile/Browse** button in the GWT development shell window. This will compile the application and launch the application in a separate web-browser window.

All this dynamic JavaScript magic means that when you try to view the source for the application from the web browser, you will always see the HTML from the host page. This can be disconcerting when you are trying to debug problems. But the fantastic Eclipse support in GWT means that you can debug issues from the comfort of a graphical debugger by setting breakpoints and stepping through the entire application one line at a time! We will learn more about debugging of GWT applications in Chapter 8.

Summary

In this chapter we generated a new GWT application using the provided helper scripts like applicationCreator. We then generated the Eclipse support files for the project. We also created a new random quote AJAX application. We saw how to run this new application in both the hosted and web modes.

In the next chapter, we are going to learn how to create GWT services that will enable us to provide asynchronous functionality that can be accessed via AJAX from the GWT application web pages.

3
Creating Services

In this chapter, we will learn how to create services, which is the GWT term for providing server-side functionality. The term **service**, as used in the GWT context does not bear any relation to a web service. It refers to the code that the client invokes on the server side in order to access the functionality provided by the server. Most of the applications that we develop will require access to a server to retrieve some data or information, and then display it to the user in an intuitive and non-intrusive way using AJAX. The best way in a GWT application to accomplish this is through a service.

In this chapter we will go through the necessary steps for creating services. We will first create the various artifacts required for creating a simple `Prime Number` service that verifies if the provided number is a prime number. The application is trivial but the concepts apply to any GWT service that you will create. We are also going to create a simple client that will consume the `Prime Number` service.

The tasks that we will address are:

- Creating a service definition interface
- Creating an asynchronous service definition interface
- Creating a service implementation
- Consuming the service

The first three tasks need to be done for every GWT service that you create.

Creating a Service Definition Interface

A service definition interface acts as a contract between the client and the server. This interface will be implemented by the actual service that we build later on in this chapter. It defines the functionality that is to be provided by the service, and lays down the ground rules for clients wanting to consume the functionality provided by this service.

Time for Action—Creating a Prime Number Service

We will create the definition for our Prime Number service. We will also create a new project called `Samples` to contain the code we create in this chapter and the rest of the book.

1. Create a new Eclipse GWT project named `Samples` using the `projectCreator` and `applicationCreator`. Specify the name of the application class as `com.packtpub.gwtbook.samples.client.Samples`.

2. Import the newly created project into the Eclipse IDE.

3. Create a new Java file named `PrimesService.java` in the `com.packtpub.gwtbook.samples.client` package. Define a `PrimesService` interface with one method that verifies if a number is a prime number. It takes an integer as a parameter and returns a Boolean value upon verification:

```
public interface PrimesService extends RemoteService
{
  public boolean isPrimeNumber(int numberToVerify);
}
```

What Just Happened?

The `PrimesService` is a service definition interface. It specifies the supported method, and the parameters that should be passed to it, in order for the service to return a response. The term RPC in the GWT context refers to a mechanism for easily passing Java objects between a client and the server via the HTTP protocol. The GWT framework does this automatically for us, as long as we use only the supported types for our method parameters and return values. Currently, the following Java types and objects are supported by GWT:

* Primitive types—character, byte, short, integer, long, Boolean, float, and double
* Primitive type wrapper classes—character, byte, short, integer, long, Boolean, float, and double
* String
* Date
* Arrays of any of these `serializable` types
* Custom classes implementing the `isSerializable` interface, and whose non-transient fields are one of the above supported types

You can also use collections of the supported object types as method parameters and return types. However, in order to use them, you need to explicitly mention the type of objects they are expected to contain by utilizing a special Javadoc annotation @ gwt.typeArgs. For instance, here is how we would define a service method that takes a list of integers as input parameters, and returns a list of strings:

```
public interface MyRPCService extends RemoteService
{
  /*
   * @gwt.typeArgs numbers <java.lang.Integer>
   * @gwt.typeArgs <java.lang.String>
   */
    List myServiceMethod(List numbers);
}
```

The first annotation indicates that this method accepts only a parameter that is a list of integer objects, and the second annotation indicates that the return parameter from this method is a list of string objects.

Creating an Asynchronous Service Definition Interface

The interface created in the previous task is a synchronous one. In order to take advantage of the AJAX support in GWT, we will need to create the asynchronous version of this interface, which will be used for making remote calls in the background to the server.

Time for Action—Utilizing the AJAX Support

In this section, we will create an asynchronous version of the service definition interface.

Create a new Java file named PrimesServiceAsync.java in the com.packtpub. gwtbook.samples.client package. Define a PrimesServiceAsync interface:

```
public interface PrimesServiceAsync
{
  public void isPrimeNumber(inr numberToVerify, AsyncCallbackcallback);
}
```

What Just Happened?

The asynchronous version of our service definition interface must have the same methods as the synchronous interface, except for the requirement that all of its methods must have an `AsyncCallback` object as a parameter, and the methods may not return anything. The callback object acts as the binding between the client and the server. Once an asynchronous call is made by the client, the notification, when the call completes its processing on the server side is made through this callback object. Essentially this makes the AJAX magic happen! You do not have to do anything special for all this magic to happen, other than making sure that you provide this asynchronous interface for your service definition. The GWT framework will automatically take care of all the communication between the client and the server. A client application that is using this service will invoke the service through this method, passing it a callback object and will automatically be notified of either success through a callback to the `onSuccess()` method in the client application or failure through a callback to the `onFailure()` method in the client application. The current release of GWT only supports making an asynchronous call back to the server. Even though the service definition interface is synchronous, that does not mean that you can use it to make a synchronous call to the server. So any service that you build using GWT can currently only be accessed asynchronously via AJAX.

Creating a Service Implementation

We have so far created the interfaces that define the functionality of our Prime Number service. In this section, we are going to start implementing and filling out the service class and create the actual implementation of the Prime Number service.

Time for Action—Implement Our Service

We are going to create the implementation of the Prime Number service. It checks to see if the provided number is a prime number by ensuring that it is only divisible by one and itself. The verification result is returned as a Boolean value.

Create a new Java file, named `PrimesServiceImpl.java` in the `com.packtpub.gwtbook.samples.server` package. Define a `PrimesServiceImpl` class that extends `RemoteServiceServlet` and implements the previously created `PrimesService` interface. Add functionality to this class to verify if the provided number is a prime number.

```
public class PrimesServiceImpl extends RemoteServiceServlet
                                          implements PrimesService
{
  private static final long serialVersionUID = -8620968747002510678L;
```

```
public boolean isPrimeNumber(int numberToVerify)
{
  boolean isPrime = true;
  int limit = (int) Math.sqrt ( numberToVerify );
  for ( int i = 2; i <= limit; i++ )
  {
    if(numberToVerify % i == 0 )
    {
      isPrime = false;
      break;
    }
  }
  return isPrime;
}
}
```

What Just Happened?

Since this is the implementation of the Prime Number service, this class needs to implement the service definition interface, and add functionality to the implemented methods. This task and the previous tasks delineate the steps that are always required in order to create a GWT service. Creating and using RPC services is a critical step on the path to unlocking the power of GWT and for using it efficiently and effectively. The basic architecture of a GWT application consists of a client-side user interface that is rendered in a web browser and interacts with the server-side functionality implemented as an RPC service to asynchronously retrieve data and information without refreshing the page. The service in a GWT application wraps the server-side model of an application, and thus usually maps to the role of a model in the MVC architecture.

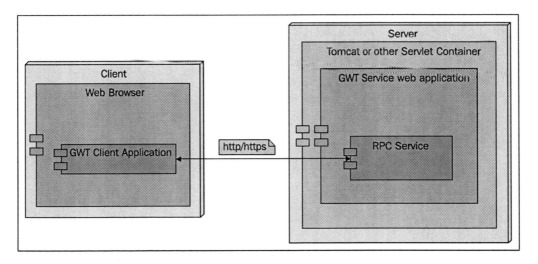

Let us look at the relationships between the various classes and interfaces that we are creating for a service. Every time we create an RPC service we utilize some GWT framework classes, and create some new classes and interfaces. Here are the classes and interfaces that are created after completion of the above task:

- `PrimesService`: Our service definition interface. It defines the methods in our service and extends the `RemoteService` marker interface that indicates that this is a GWT RPC service. This is the synchronous definition and the server-side implementation must implement this interface.

- `PrimesServiceAsync`: The asynchronous definition of our interface. It must have the same methods as the synchronous interface, except for the requirement that all of its methods must have an `AsyncCallback` object as a parameter and the methods may not return anything. The naming convention recommended for this interface is to suffix the name of our synchronous interface with the word `Async`.

- `PrimesServiceImpl`: This is the server-side implementation of our service. This must extend `RemoteServiceServlet` and implement our synchronous interface — `PrimesService`.

GWT framework classes used by us to create the `PrimesService`:

- `RemoteService`: A marker interface that should be implemented by all the RPC services.

- `RemoteServiceServlet`: The `PrimesServiceImpl` service implementation class extends this class and adds the required functionality. This class provides support for serializing and deserializing requests, and ensures that the requests invoke the right method in the `PrimesServiceImpl` class.

Here is a diagram depicting the relationship between the various classes and interfaces that were involved in creating the Prime Number service.

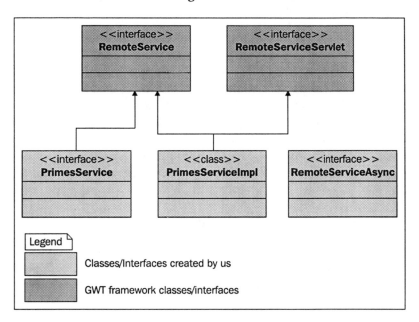

Our service implementation extends the RemoteServiceServlet, which inherits from the HttpServlet class. The RemoteServiceServlet takes care of automatically deserializing incoming requests and serializing the outgoing responses. GWT probably opted to use the servlet-based approach because it is simple and is well known and used in the Java community. It also makes it easy to move our service implementation between any servlet containers, and opens the door to a wide variety of integration possibilities between GWT and other frameworks. This has been used by several members of the GWT community to implement integration between GWT and other frameworks such as Struts and Spring. The RPC wire format used by GWT is loosely based on the JavaScript Object Notation (JSON). This protocol is proprietary to GWT and it is currently undocumented. However, the RemoteServiceServlet provides two methods — onAfterResponseSerialized() and onBeforeRequestDeserialized(), which you can override to inspect and print out the serialized request and response.

The basic pattern and architecture for creating any GWT service is always the same and consists of these basic steps:

1. Create a service definition interface.
2. Create an asynchronous version of the service definition interface.

3. Create the service implementation class. In the service implementation class we access the functionality provided by the external service and convert the results to match our requirements.

In the next section, we will create a simple client that consumes this new service. We will learn about deploying this service to external servlet containers such as Tomcat in Chapter 10. The concepts from this example are applicable to every GWT service that we create. We will create at least these two interfaces and an implementation class for every service that we create. This will help us to provide server functionality that can be accessed in an asynchronous way by a GWT client. The service that we have created above is independent of the GWT client application, and can be used by multiple applications. We only need to ensure that we register the service correctly in a servlet container, so that it can be accessed by our client applications.

Consuming the Service

We have completed implementing the Prime Number service. Now we are going to create a simple client that can consume the `PrimesService`. This will help us test the functionality of the service to ensure that it does things that it is supposed to do.

Time for Action—Creating the Client

We will create a simple client that will connect to the Prime Number service and check if a given number is a prime number. We will add a text box for typing in the number to check, and a button that will invoke the service when clicked. It will display the results of the call in an alert dialog.

1. Create the client in a new file named `PrimesClient.java` in the `com.packtpub.gwtbook.samples.client` package that extends the `EntryPoint` class.

```
public class PrimesClient implements EntryPoint
{
}
```

2. Add an `onModuleLoad()` method to this new class, and create a text box.

```
public void onModuleLoad()
{
   final TextBox primeNumber = new TextBox();
}
```

3. Instantiate the `PrimesService` and store it in a variable in the
    `onModuleLoad()` method.

```
final PrimesServiceAsync primesService =
                              (PrimesServiceAsync) GWT
GWT.create(PrimesService.class);
ServiceDefTarget endpoint = (ServiceDefTarget) primesService;
endpoint.setServiceEntryPoint(GWT.getModuleBaseURL()+"primes");
```

4. Create a new button, and add an event handler to listen for clicks on the
    button. In the handler, invoke the `PrimesService` using the text typed into
    the text box as the input parameter to the service. Display the result in an
    alert dialog.

```
final Button checkPrime=new Button("Is this a prime number?",
                                    new ClickListener()
{
  public void onClick(Widget sender)
  {
    AsyncCallback callback = new AsyncCallback()
    {
      public void onSuccess(Object result)
      {
        if(((Boolean) result).booleanValue())
        {
          Window.alert("Yes, "+ primeNumber.getText()
                              + "' is a prime number.");
        }
        else
        {
          Window.alert("No, "+ primeNumber.getText()
                              + "' is not a prime number.");
        }
      }
      public void onFailure(Throwable caught)
      {
        Window.alert("Error while calling the Primes
                                      Service.");
      }
    };
    primesService.isPrimeNumber(Integer
                parseInt(primeNumber.getText()), callback);
  }
});
```

5. Add the following entry to the application's `module.xml` file in order for the client to find this service.

```
<servlet path="/primes" class=
        "com.packtpub.gwtbook.samples.server.PrimesServiceImpl"/>
```

Here is the client. Type in a number, and click the button to check if the number is a prime number.

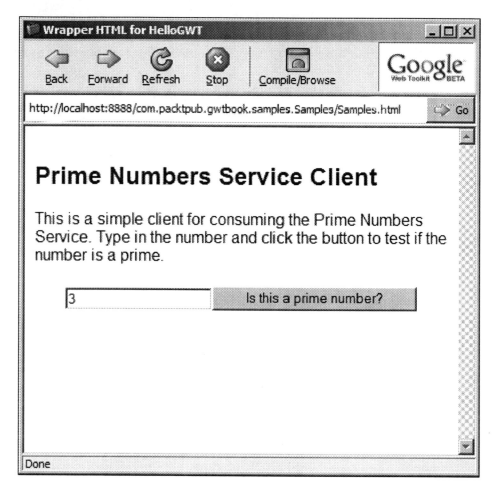

The response is displayed in an alert dialog as shown below:

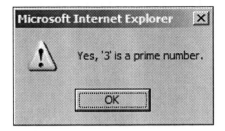

What Just Happened?

The Prime Number service client invokes the service, by passing in the required parameter to the PrimesService. We make an entry for the service in the module. xml file so that the GWT framework can initialize things correctly and the client can find the service. We have followed a common pattern for creating simple clients that consume GWT services:

1. Create a class that implements the EntryPoint class.

2. Override the onModuleLoad() method to add the desired user-interface widgets.

3. Add an event handler to one of the user interface widgets to invoke the service when the handler is triggered.

4. In the event handler, handle the callbacks for success and failure of the call to the service method, and take some action with the results of the call.

5. Add an entry to the GWT application module.xml for the service to be consumed.

We will use this common pattern along with some variations when creating sample applications throughout this book.

Summary

In this chapter we took a look at creating the various classes and interfaces that are required as part of creating a new Prime Number GWT service. We also created a client that can consume the prime number service.

In the next chapter, we are going to create interactive web user interfaces using GWT.

4
Interactive Forms

In this chapter, we will learn different ways of creating interactive forms, which utilize GWT and AJAX to provide a much smoother user experience when using web-based user interfaces. This chapter along with the next two chapters is going to provide the foundation for our exploration of GWT.

The tasks that we will address are:

1. Live search
2. Password strength checker
3. Auto fill forms
4. Sortable tables
5. Dynamic lists
6. Flickr-style editable labels

Sample Application

We are going to incorporate all of the sample applications that we are creating in this book into the Samples GWT application that we created in the previous chapter. We will be doing this in a style that is similar to the KitchenSink application that we explored in Chapter 1. In order to do this, we will follow the steps given below:

- The user interface for the application will be created in a class that extends the SamplePanel class in the com.packtpub.gwtbook.samples.client package.

- This class will then be initialized and added to the list of applications in the Samples class in the com.packtpub.gwtbook.samples.client package. Since the Samples class is set up as the entry point class, when GWT starts up, it will load this class and display all of the sample applications, just like the KitchenSink.

The source code for all the samples is available from the download site for the book. Please see the Appendix for instructions on downloading and running the samples.

Live Search

`Live Search` is a user interface that actively provides the user with choices matching the search criteria that the user types in. It is a very popular AJAX pattern that is used to continuously display all valid results to a user as the user refines the search query. Since the user's query is constantly synchronized with the displayed results, it creates a very smooth search experience for the user. It also enables the user to easily experiment with different search queries very quickly in a highly interactive fashion. The results from the search are asynchronously retrieved from the server without any page refreshes or resubmission of search criteria. The Google search page (`http://google.com/`) uses this to great effect. It even tells you the number of search results that match your query as you type!

Instant feedback of the kind provided by the `Live Search` AJAX pattern could also be harnessed to pre-fetch results from server and use them for anticipating the user's actions. This kind of an instantaneous response smoothens the user experience of the application and significantly improves the application latency. Google Maps (`http://maps.google.com/`) are nice examples of using this pattern to pre-fetch the map data as you are navigating around the map.

Time for Action—Search as you Type!

In this `Live Search` example, we will create an application that retrieves a list of fruit names that begin with the letters that you type into the search text. You can refine your query criteria by reducing or increasing the number of letters that you type, and the user interface will display the matching result set in real time.

1. Create a new Java file named `LiveSearchService.java` in the `com.packtpub.gwtbook.samples.client` package. Define a `LiveSearchService` interface with one method to retrieve the search results matching the string provided as a parameter to the method.

   ```
   public interface LiveSearchService extends RemoteService
   {
     public List getCompletionItems(String itemToMatch);
   }
   ```

2. Create the asynchronous version of this service definition interface in a new Java file named `LiveSearchServiceAsync.java` in the `com.packtpub.gwtbook.samples.client` package:

```
public interface LiveSearchServiceAsync
{
  public void getCompletionItems
                 (String itemToMatch, AsyncCallback callback);
}
```

3. Create the implementation of our live search service in a new Java file named `LiveSearchServiceImpl.java` in the `com.packtpub.gwtbook.samples.server` package. We will create a string array that holds a list of fruits and when the service method is invoked we will return a sub-list of fruits from this array whose names start with the string provided as a parameter.

```
public class LiveSearchServiceImpl extends RemoteServiceServlet
                                     implements LiveSearchService
{
  private String[] items = new String[]
  {"apple", "peach", "orange", "banana", "plum", "avocado",
     "strawberry", "pear", "watermelon", "pineapple", "grape",
                                   "blueberry", "cantaloupe"
  };
  public List getCompletionItems(String itemToMatch)
  {
    ArrayList completionList = new ArrayList();
    for (int i = 0; i < items.length; i++)
    {
      if (items[i].startsWith(itemToMatch.toLowerCase()))
      {
        completionList.add(items[i]);
      }
    }
    return completionList;
  }
}
```

4. Our server-side implementation is complete. Now we will create the user interface for interacting with the live search service. Create a new Java file named `LiveSearchPanel.java` in the `com.packtpub.gwtbook.samples.client.panels` package that extends the `com.packtpub.gwtbook.samples.client.panels.SamplePanel` class. As mentioned at the beginning of this chapter, each of the user interfaces created in this book will be added to a sample application that is similar to the `KitchenSink` application that is available as one of the sample projects with the GWT download. That is why we will create each user interface as a panel that extends the `SamplePanel` class, and we will add the created panel to the list of samples panels in the sample application. Add a text box for typing in the search string, and a `FlexTable` that will display the matching items retrieved from the service. Finally, create an instance of the `LiveSearchService` that we are going to invoke.

    ```java
    public FlexTable liveResultsPanel = new FlexTable();
    public TextBox searchText = new TextBox();
    final LiveSearchServiceAsync
    liveSearchService=(LiveSearchServiceAsync)
    GWT.create(LiveSearchService.class);
    ```

5. In the constructor for the `LiveSearchPanel`, create the service target and set its entry point. Also create a new `VerticalPanel` that we will use as the container for the widgets that we are adding to the user interface. Set the CSS style for the search text box. This style is defined in the `Samples.css` file, and is part of the source code distribution package for this book. Please see the Appendix for details on how to download the source code package.

    ```java
    ServiceDefTarget endpoint=(ServiceDefTarget) liveSearchService;
    endpoint.setServiceEntryPoint("/Samples/livesearch");
    VerticalPanel workPanel = new VerticalPanel();
    searchText.setStyleName("liveSearch-TextBox");
    ```

6. In the same constructor, add a listener to the text box that will call the `LiveSearchService` asynchronously as the user types in the text box, and update the pop-up panel continuously with the latest results matching the current string in the text box. This is the method that starts of all the magic by calling the service to get a list of completion items.

    ```java
    searchText.addKeyboardListener(new KeyboardListener()
    {
      public void onKeyPress
                    (Widget sender, char keyCode, int modifiers)
      {
        // not implemented
      }
    ```

```
    public void onKeyDown
                    (Widget sender, char keyCode, int modifiers)
    {
      for (int i = 0; i < liveResultsPanel.getRowCount(); i++)
      {
        liveResultsPanel.removeRow(i);
      }
    }
    public void onKeyUp
                    (Widget sender, char keyCode, int modifiers)
    {
      for (int i = 0; i < liveResultsPanel.getRowCount(); i++)
      {
        liveResultsPanel.removeRow(i);
      }
      if (searchText.getText().length() > 0)
      {
        AsyncCallback callback = new AsyncCallback()
        {
          public void onSuccess(Object result)
          {
            ArrayList resultItems = (ArrayList) result;
            int row = 0;
            for(Iterator iter=resultItems.iterator();
                                            iter.hasNext();)
            {
              liveResultsPanel.setText
                          (row++, 0, (String) iter.next());
            }
          }
          public void onFailure(Throwable caught)
          {
            Window.alert("Live search failed because "
                                    + caught.getMessage());
          }
        };
        liveSearchService.getCompletionItems
                            (searchText.getText(),callback);
      }
    }
  });
```

7. Finally, in the constructor, add the search text box and the search results panel to the work panel. Create a little info panel that displays descriptive text about this application, so that we can display this text when this sample is selected in the list of available samples in our `Samples` application. Add the info panel and the work panel to a dock panel, and initialize the widget.

```
liveResultsPanel.setStyleName("liveSearch-Results");
HorizontalPanel infoPanel = new HorizontalPanel();
infoPanel.add(new HTML
            ("<div class='infoProse'>Type the first few letters
            of the name of a fruit in the text box below. A
            list of fruits with names starting with the typed
            letters will be displayed. The list is retrieved
            from the server asynchronously. This is nice AJAX
            pattern for providing user-friendly search
            functionality in an application.</div>"));
workPanel.add(searchText);
workPanel.add(liveResultsPanel);
DockPanel workPane = new DockPanel();
workPane.add(infoPanel, DockPanel.NORTH);
workPane.add(workPanel, DockPanel.CENTER);
workPane.setCellHeight(workPanel, "100%");
workPane.setCellWidth(workPanel, "100%");
initWidget(workPane);
```

8. Add the service to the module file for the `Samples` application—`Samples.gwt.xml` in the `com.packtpub.gwtbook.samples` package. Adding this path to the module file let us create and set the endpoint information for this service using this path.

```
<servlet path="/livesearch" class=
  "com.packtpub.gwtbook.samples.server.LiveSearchServiceImpl"/>
```

Here is the user interface for the application:

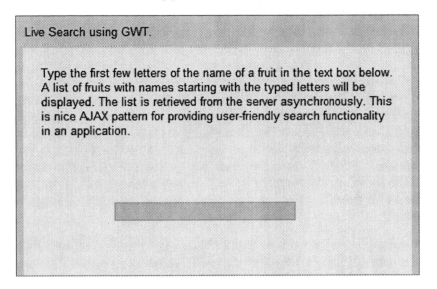

Once you start typing in the first few letters of a fruit name, all the names of the fruits whose name starts with the string typed in are retrieved and displayed in a panel below the text box.

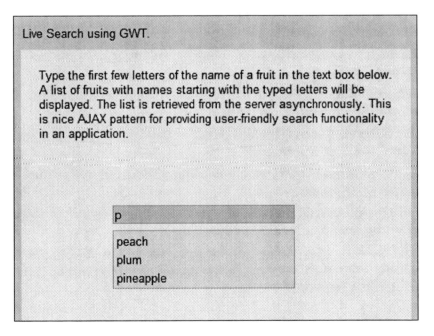

What Just Happened?

The user interface for the application displays a text box when you load the application in the browser. When you type a letter in the box, the onKeyUp() event will be triggered on the text box and in this event handler we asynchronously call the getCompletionItems() in the LiveSearchService with the text that is currently in the text box. The implementation of this method in our service returns a list with all the matching names. The matching names in this example are retrieved from a map contained in the service itself, but could just as easily be retrieved from a database, another application or a web service, depending on your application needs. We add the items that are present in the list to a FlexTable widget, which is present right below the text box. A FlexTable allows us to create tables that can be dynamically expanded. If the text box is empty or if we delete all the text in the box, then we clear out the list in the table. We use a panel as the container for all of the widgets in this application.

Panels are containers for widgets in the GWT framework and are used for laying them out. You can add any widget or even other panels to a panel. This enables us to build complex user interfaces by combining widgets together by adding them to panels. The commonly used panels in the GWT framework are:

- **DockPanel**: A panel that lays out the child widgets that are added to it by docking them or positioning them at the edges, and it allows the last added widget to take the remaining space.

- **CellPanel**: A panel that lays out its widgets within the cells of a table.

- **TabPanel**: A panel that lays out the child widgets in a tabbed set of pages, each with a widget.

- **HorizontalPanel**: A panel that lays out all of its child widgets in a single horizontal column from left to right.

- **VerticalPanel**: A panel that lays out all of its child widgets in a single vertical column from top to bottom.

- **FlowPanel**: A panel that lays out its widgets from left to right just like text flowing across a line.

- **PopupPanel**: A panel that displays its child widgets by popping up or overlaying over other widgets on the page.

- **StackPanel**: A panel that lays out its child widgets by stacking them vertically from top to bottom. The metaphor used is the same as the user interface of Microsoft Outlook.

We will be using most of these panels to lay out our user interfaces in this chapter and the rest of this book. The concepts from this task can be extended and applied to almost any type of search that you want to provide to your users in your application. You can even enhance and extend this application to provide further information to the user such as the number of matching results. The plumbing and tools provided by GWT make it extremely easy to provide this functionality. One of the best examples of the live search AJAX pattern and its use is the Google suggest service. As you type a search query string in a text field, it retrieves and displays a list of matching results in a continuous fashion. You can see it in action at `http://www.google.com/webhp?complete=1&hl=en`.

Password Strength Checker

Visual cues are great way to inform the user of the status of things in the application. Message boxes and alerts are used much too often for this purpose, but they usually end up irritating the user. A much smoother and enjoyable user experience is provided by subtly indicating to the user the status as an application is used. In this section, we are going to create an application that indicates the strength of a typed password to the user by the use of colors and checkboxes. We are going to use check-boxes very differently than their normal usage. This is an example of using GWT widgets in new and different ways, and mixing and matching them to provide a great user experience.

Time for Action—Creating the Checker

In the current day and age, passwords are required for almost everything, and choosing secure passwords is very important. There are numerous criteria suggested for creating a password that is secure from most common password cracking exploits. These criteria run the gamut from creating 15 letter passwords with a certain number of lower case and numeric digits to creating passwords using random password generators. In our example application, we are going to create a password strength checker that is very simple, and only checks the number of letters in the password. A password string that contains less than five letters will be considered weak, while a password that contains between five and seven letters will be considered to be of medium strength. Any password containing more than seven letters will be considered as strong. The criteria were deliberately kept simple so that we can focus on creating the application without getting all tangled up in the actual password strength criteria. This will help us to understand the concepts and then you can extend it to use any password strength criteria that your application warrants. This example uses a service to get the password strength, but this could also be done all on the client without needing to use a server.

1. Create a new Java file named `PasswordStrengthService.java` in the `com.packtpub.gwtbook.samples.client` package. Define a `PasswordStrengthService` interface with one method to retrieve the strength of a password string provided as a parameter to the method:

```
public interface PasswordStrengthService extends RemoteService
{
  public int checkStrength(String password);
}
```

2. Create the asynchronous version of this service definition interface in a new Java file named `PasswordStrengthServiceAsync.java` in the `com.packtpub.gwtbook.samples.client` package :

```
public interface PasswordStrengthServiceAsync
{
  public void checkStrength
                     (String password, AsyncCallback callback);
}
```

3. Create the implementation of our password strength service in a new Java file named `PasswordStrengthServiceImpl.java` in the `com.packtpub.gwtbook.samples.server` package.

```
public class PasswordStrengthServiceImpl extends
      RemoteServiceServlet  implements PasswordStrengthService
{
  private int STRONG = 9;
  private int MEDIUM = 6;
  private int WEAK = 3;
  public int checkStrength(String password)
  {
    if (password.length() <= 4)
    {
      return WEAK;
    }
    else if (password.length() < 8)
    {
      return MEDIUM;
    }else
    {
      return STRONG;
    }
  }
}
```

4. Now let's create the user interface for this application. Create a new Java
    file named `PasswordStrengthPanel.java` in the `com.packtpub.gwtbook.`
    `samples.client.panels` package that extends the `com.packtpub.gwtbook.`
    `samples.client.panels.SamplePanel` class. Create a text box for entering
    the password string an `ArrayList` named `strengthPanel` for holding the
    checkboxes that we will use for displaying the strength of the password. Also
    create the `PasswordStrengthService` object.

    ```
    public TextBox passwordText = new TextBox();
    final PasswordStrengthServiceAsync pwStrengthService =
                              (PasswordStrengthServiceAsync)
                    GWT.create(PasswordStrengthService.class);
    public ArrayList strength = new ArrayList();
    ```

5. Add a private method for clearing all the checkboxes by setting their style to
    the default style.

    ```
    private void clearStrengthPanel()
    {
      for (Iterator iter = strength.iterator(); iter.hasNext();)
      {
        ((CheckBox) iter.next()).
                          setStyleName(getPasswordStrengthStyle(0));
      }
    }
    ```

6. Add a private method that will return the CSS name, based on the password
    strength. This is a nice way for us to dynamically set the style for the
    checkbox, based on the strength.

    ```
    private String getPasswordStrengthStyle(int passwordStrength)
    {
      if (passwordStrength == 3)
      {
        return "pwStrength-Weak";
      }
      else if (passwordStrength == 6)
      {
        return "pwStrength-Medium";
      }
      else if (passwordStrength == 9)
      {
        return "pwStrength-Strong";
      }
    ```

```
        else
        {
          return "";
        }
  }
```

7. In the constructor for the `PasswordStrengthPanel` class, create a `HorizontalPanel` named `strengthPanel`, add nine checkboxes to it, and set its style. As mentioned before the styles that we are using in the sample applications in this book are available in the file `Samples.css`, which is part of the source code distribution for this book. We also add these same checkboxes to the `strength` object, so that we can retrieve them later to set their state. These checkboxes will be used for displaying the password strength visually. Create a new `VerticalPanel` that we will use as the container for the widgets that we are adding to the user interface. Finally, create the service target and set its entry point.

```
HorizontalPanel strengthPanel = new HorizontalPanel();
strengthPanel.setStyleName("pwStrength-Panel");
for (int i = 0; i < 9; i++)
  {
     CheckBox singleBox = new CheckBox();
     strengthPanel.add(singleBox);
    strength.add(singleBox);
  }
VerticalPanel workPanel = new VerticalPanel();
ServiceDefTarget endpoint=(ServiceDefTarget) pwStrengthService;
endpoint.setServiceEntryPoint(GWT.getModuleBaseURL() +
                                            "pwstrength");
```

8. In the same constructor, set the style for the password text box, and add an event handler to listen for changes to the password box.

```
passwordText.setStyleName("pwStrength-Textbox");
passwordText.addKeyboardListener(new KeyboardListener()
  {
  public void onKeyDown
                  (Widget sender, char keyCode, int modifiers)
    {
    }
  public void onKeyPress
                  (Widget sender, char keyCode, int modifiers)
    {
    }
  public void onKeyUp(Widget sender, char keyCode,
                                            int modifiers)
    {
```

```
      if (passwordText.getText().length() > 0)
      {
        AsyncCallback callback = new AsyncCallback()
        {
          public void onSuccess(Object result)
          {
            clearStrengthPanel();
            int checkedStrength = ((Integer) result).intValue();
            for (int i = 0; i < checkedStrength; i++)
            {
              ((CheckBox) strength.get(i)).setStyleName
                    (getPasswordStrengthStyle(checkedStrength));
            }
          }
          public void onFailure(Throwable caught)
            {
              Window.alert("Error calling the password strength
                            service." + caught.getMessage());
            }
        };
        pwStrengthService.checkStrength
                      (passwordText.getText(), callback);
      }
      else
      {
        clearStrengthPanel();
      }
    }
  });
```

9. Finally, in the constructor, add the password text box and the strength panel to the work panel. Create a little info panel that displays descriptive text about this application, so that we can display this text when this sample is selected in the list of available samples in our Samples application. Add the info panel and the work panel to a dock panel, and initialize the widget.

```
HorizontalPanel infoPanel = new HorizontalPanel();
infoPanel.add(new HTML(
        "<div class='infoProse'>Start typing a password
        string. The strength of the password will be
        checked and displayed below. Red indicates that the
        password is Weak, Orange indicates a Medium
        strength password and Green indicates a Strong
        password. The algorithm for checking the strength
        is very basic and checks the length of the password
        string.</div>"));
workPanel.add(passwordText);
```

```
workPanel.add(infoPanel);
workPanel.add(strengthPanel);
DockPanel workPane = new DockPanel();
workPane.add(infoPanel, DockPanel.NORTH);
workPane.add(workPanel, DockPanel.CENTER);
workPane.setCellHeight(workPanel, "100%");
workPane.setCellWidth(workPanel, "100%");
initWidget(workPane);
```

10. Add the service to the module file for the `Samples` application—`Samples.gwt.xml` in the `com.packtpub.gwtbook.samples` package.

```
<servlet path="/pwstrength" class=
                    "com.packtpub.gwtbook.samples.server.
                        PasswordStrengthServiceImpl"/>
```

Here is the user interface for the password strength checking application:

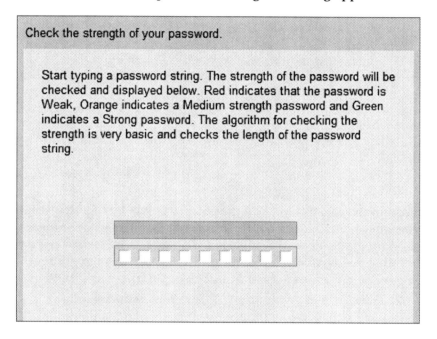

Now start typing a password string to check its strength. Here is the password strength when you type a password string that is less than five characters:

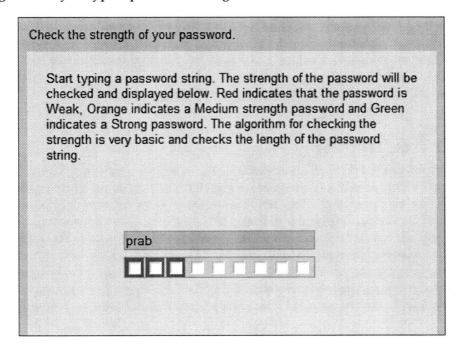

What Just Happened?

The password strength service checks the size of the provided string and returns an integer value of three, six, or nine based on whether it is weak, medium, or strong. It makes this determination by using the criteria that if the password string is less than five characters in length, it is weak, and if it is more than five characters but not greater than seven characters, it is considered a medium strength password. Anything over seven characters is considered to be a strong password.

The user interface consists of a text box for entering a password string and a panel containing nine checkboxes that visually displays the strength of the typed string as a password. An event handler is registered to listen for keyboard events generated by the password text box. Whenever the password text changes, which happens when we type into the field or change a character in the field, we communicate asynchronously with the password strength service and retrieve the strength of the given string as a password. The returned strength is displayed to the user in a visual fashion by the use of colors to symbolize the three different password strengths.

The password strength is displayed in a compound widget that is created by adding nine checkboxes to a `HorizontalPanel`. The color of the checkboxes is changed using CSS depending on the strength of the password string. This process of combining the basic widgets provided by GWT into more complex widgets to build user interfaces is a common pattern in building GWT applications. It is possible to build quite intricate user interfaces in this way by utilizing the power of the GWT framework. We will see more examples of this as we continue to explore various GWT applications later in this chapter and also throughout this book.

Auto Form Fill

Forms are ubiquitous on the Web and are widely used for everything from displaying information from customer profiles to filling out applications online. We do not like going through all those fields and typing in the information in every time, especially if we have already done this on that site once before. A very nice way to speed this up would be to pre-populate the fields with the previously collected information when a key form field is filled in. This not only saves the customer some typing, it also is a great usability enhancement that improves the whole customer experience. In this section, we are going to build a form that will automatically fill out the various fields when we type in a recognized value in the Customer ID field.

Time for Action—Creating a Dynamic Form

We are going to create an application that makes it easy to fill out the various fields of a form when a certain value is provided in one of the fields. This is a very common occurrence in most of the web-based business applications where, for instance, user information needs to be provided in order to register for a service. In the case of a new user, this information will need to be filled out by the user, but in the case of a previous user of the system, this information is already available and can be accessed and used for filling out all the fields when the user types in a unique identifier that identifies him or her, an ID of some sort. In this application we are going to automatically fill out the various fields of the form when a user enters in a `CustomerID` that is known to us.

1. Create a new Java file named `AutoFormFillService.java` in the `com.packtpub.gwtbook.samples.client` package. Define an `AutoFormFillService` interface with one method to retrieve the form information when provided a key:

   ```
   public interface AutoFormFillService extends RemoteService
   {
     public HashMap getFormInfo(String formKey);
   }
   ```

2. Create a new Java file named `AutoFormFillServiceAsync.java` in the `com.packtpub.gwtbook.samples.client` package. Define a `AutoFormFillAsync` interface:

```
public interface AutoFormFillServiceAsync
{
  public void getFormInfo
                  (String formKey, AsyncCallback callback);
}
```

3. Create a new Java file named `AutoFormFillServiceImpl.java` in the `com.packtpub.gwtbook.samples.server` package. Define a `AutoFormFillServiceImpl` class that extends `RemoteServiceServlet` and implements the previously created `AutoFormFillService` interface. First we will use a simple `HashMap` to store the customer information and add a method to populate the map. In your application you can retrieve this customer information from any external data source, such as a database.

```
private HashMap formInfo = new HashMap();
private void loadCustomerData()
{
  HashMap customer1 = new HashMap();
  customer1.put("first name", "Joe");
  customer1.put("last name", "Customer");
  customer1.put("address", "123 peachtree street");
  customer1.put("city", "Atlanta");
  customer1.put("state", "GA");
  customer1.put("zip", "30339");
  customer1.put("phone", "770-123-4567");
  formInfo.put("1111", customer1);
  HashMap customer2 = new HashMap();
  customer2.put("first name", "Jane");
  customer2.put("last name", "Customer");
  customer2.put("address", "456 elm street");
  customer2.put("city", "Miami");
  customer2.put("state", "FL");
  customer2.put("zip", "24156");
  customer2.put("phone", "817-123-4567");
  formInfo.put("2222", customer2);
  HashMap customer3 = new HashMap();
  customer3.put("first name", "Jeff");
  customer3.put("last name", "Customer");
  customer3.put("address", "789 sunset blvd");
  customer3.put("city", "Los Angeles");
  customer3.put("state", "CA");
```

```
        customer3.put("zip", "90211");
        customer3.put("phone", "714-478-9802");
        formInfo.put("3333", customer3);
    }
```

4. Add logic to the `getFormInfo()` to return the form information for a provided form key. We take the provided key that was entered in the form by the user, and use that to look up the user information, and return it asynchronously to the client application.

```java
public HashMap getFormInfo(String formKey)
{
    if (formInfo.containsKey(formKey))
    {
        return (HashMap) formInfo.get(formKey);
    }
    else
    {
        return new HashMap();
    }
}
```

5. Create the user interface for this application in a new Java file named `AutoFormFillPanel.java` in the `com.packtpub.gwtbook.samples.client.panels` package. Create a text box, and a label for each information field.

```java
private TextBox custID = new TextBox();
private TextBox firstName = new TextBox();
private TextBox lastName = new TextBox();
private TextBox address = new TextBox();
private TextBox zip = new TextBox();
private TextBox phone = new TextBox();
private TextBox city = new TextBox();
private TextBox state = new TextBox();
private Label custIDLbl = new Label("Customer ID : ");
private Label firstNameLbl = new Label("First Name : ");
private Label lastNameLbl = new Label("Last Name : ");
private Label addressLbl = new Label("Address : ");
private Label zipLbl = new Label("Zip Code : ");
private Label phoneLbl = new Label("Phone Number : ");
private Label cityLbl = new Label("City : ");
private Label stateLbl = new Label("State : ");
HorizontalPanel itemPanel = new HorizontalPanel();
```

6. Create the service class that we are going to invoke.

```
final AutoFormFillServiceAsync autoFormFillService =
(AutoFormFillServiceAsync) GWT.create
                           (AutoFormFillService.class);
```

7. Create private methods for setting and clearing the values of the form fields. We will use these methods from the event handlers that we will set up in the constructor.

```
private void setValues(HashMap values)
{
  if (values.size() > 0)
  {
    firstName.setText((String) values.get("first name"));
    lastName.setText((String) values.get("last name"));
    address.setText((String) values.get("address"));
    city.setText((String) values.get("city"));
    state.setText((String) values.get("state"));
    zip.setText((String) values.get("zip"));
    phone.setText((String) values.get("phone"));
  }
  else
  {
    clearValues();
  }
}
private void clearValues()
{
  firstName.setText(" ");
  lastName.setText(" ");
  address.setText(" ");
  city.setText(" ");
  state.setText(" ");
  zip.setText(" ");
  phone.setText(" ");
}
```

8. Create accessor methods for retrieving the different labels. We will use these to get the label and set its value when we retrieve information from the service.

```
public Label getAddressLbl()
{
  return addressLbl;
}
public Label getCityLbl()
```

```
  {
    return cityLbl;
  }
  public Label getCustIDLbl()
  {
    return custIDLbl;
  }
  public Label getFirstNameLbl()
  {
    return firstNameLbl;
  }
  public Label getLastNameLbl()
  {
    return lastNameLbl;
  }
  public Label getPhoneLbl()
  {
    return phoneLbl;
  }
  public Label getStateLbl()
  {
    return stateLbl;
  }
  public Label getZipLbl()
  {
    return zipLbl;
  }
```

9. Create accessor methods for retrieving the different text boxes. We will use these to get the text box and set its value when we retrieve information from the service.

```
  public TextBox getAddress()
  {
    return address;
  }
  public TextBox getCity()
  {
    return city;
  }
  public TextBox getCustID()
  {
    return custID;
  }
  public TextBox getFirstName()
```

```
{
  return firstName;
}
public TextBox getLastName()
{
  return lastName;
}
public TextBox getPhone()
{
  return phone;
}
public TextBox getState()
{
  return state;
}
public TextBox getZip()
{
  return zip;
}
```

10. In the constructor for `AutoFormFillPanel`, create a new `VerticalPanel` that we will use as the container for the widgets that we are adding to the user interface. Also, create the service target and set its entry point.

```
ServiceDefTarget endpoint = (ServiceDefTarget)
                                        autoFormFillService;
endpoint.setServiceEntryPoint("/Samples/autoformfill");
```

11. Also in the constructor, create a `HorizontalPanel` named `itemPanel` and add the widgets for each form field to it. For instance, this is how we add the `customerID` field to the `itemPanel`, set its style, and add this `itemPanel` to the `workPanel`, which is the main container that we have created earlier to hold the widgets for our user interface. You will create a new `HorizontalPanel` for each form field and add it to the `workPanel`. Repeat for each form field that we have.

```
HorizontalPanel itemPanel = new HorizontalPanel();
itemPanel.setStyleName("autoFormItem-Panel");
custIDLbl.setStyleName("autoFormItem-Label");
itemPanel.add(custIDLbl);
custID.setStyleName("autoFormItem-Textbox");
itemPanel.add(custID);
workPanel.add(itemPanel);
```

12. In the same constructor, add a keyboard listener to the cust ID text box and in the event handler invoke the service to retrieve customer information for the value typed in customer ID. Set the values of the form fields from the return value of the service call.

```
custID.addKeyboardListener(new KeyboardListener()
             {
             public void onKeyDown(Widget sender,
                        char keyCode, int modifiers)
             {
             }
             public void onKeyPress(Widget sender,
                        char keyCode, int modifiers)
             {
             }
             public void onKeyUp(Widget sender, char
                        keyCode, int modifiers)
             {
             if (custID.getText().length() > 0)
             {
               AsyncCallback callback = new
                                    AsyncCallback()
               {
                 public void onSuccess
                                    (Object result)
                 {
                   setValues((HashMap) result);
                 }
             };
             autoFormFillService.getFormInfo
                        (custID.getText(), callback);
             }
               else
               {
                 clearValues();
               }
             }
             public void onFailure(Throwable caught)
             {
             Window.alert("Error while calling the
                        Auto Form Fill service."
                        + caught.getMessage());
             }
             });
```

13. Finally, in the constructor, create a little info panel that displays descriptive text about this application, so that we can display this text when this sample is selected in the list of available samples in our Samples application. Add the info panel and the work panel to a dock panel, and initialize the widget.

```
HorizontalPanel infoPanel = new HorizontalPanel();
infoPanel.add(new HTML(
                "<div class='infoProse'>This example
                demonstrates how to automatically fill a
                form by retrieving the data from the server
                asynchronously. Start typing a customer ID
                in the provided field, and corresponding
                values for that customer are retrieved
                asynchronously from the server and the form
                filled for you.</div>"));
DockPanel workPane = new DockPanel();
workPane.add(infoPanel, DockPanel.NORTH);
workPane.add(workPanel, DockPanel.CENTER);
workPane.setCellHeight(workPanel, "100%");
workPane.setCellWidth(workPanel, "100%");
initWidget(workPane);
```

14. Add the service to the module file for the Samples application—Samples. gwt.xml in the com.packtpub.gwtbook.samples package.

```
<servlet path="/autoformfill" class=
                "com.packtpub.gwtbook.samples.server.
                      AutoFormFillServiceImpl"/>
```

Here is what the application looks like when the user types in a `CustomerID`, in this case 1111, which is known to our application:

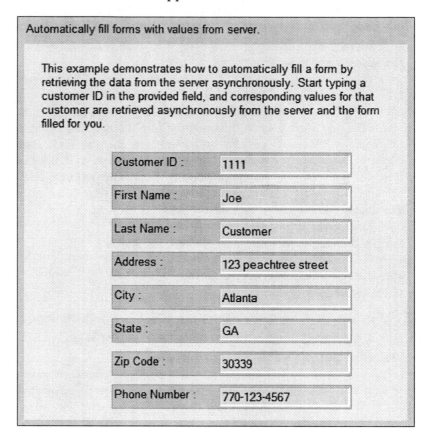

What Just Happened?

We create a service that contains customer data stored in a `HashMap` data structure. In a real application, this data would usually come from an external data source such as a database. For each customer, we create a map that contains the customer information fields stored as key value pairs. This customer map is then added to a master `HashMap` using the `customerID` as the key. This makes it easier for us to retrieve the right customer information when we are provided with the key, which in this case is the `customerID`.

```
HashMap customer2 = new HashMap();
customer2.put("first name", "Jane");
customer2.put("last name", "Customer");
customer2.put("address", "456 elm street");
customer2.put("city", "Miami");
```

```
customer2.put("state", "FL");
customer2.put("zip", "24156");
customer2.put("phone", "817-123-4567");
formInfo.put("2222", customer2);
```

When the user interface is loaded in the browser, the user is presented with a page that contains fields that are pertinent to a customer. The user needs to type a unique customer ID in the text box provided. There are only three known customer ids in this sample application—1111, 2222, and 3333. We are using the customer ID as the key to customer information here, but you could also use a social security number or any other unique ID based on the requirements of your application. Of course in a real application the user would need to enter a password as well as an ID number to avoid unauthorized display of confidential details to anyone entering a valid ID. When the user types in a customer ID in the text box, for instance 1111, the event handler `onKeyUp()` is triggered. In the event handler we invoke the `getFormInfo()` method in the `AutoFormFillService` and pass in the typed text as a parameter. The `getFormInfo()` method searches the customer information for the given customer ID and returns the information as a `HashMap`. If no information is found due to an unknown ID, we return an empty map. The values from this map are retrieved and the corresponding fields are filled in by calling the `setValues()`.

```
firstName.setText((String) values.get("first name"));
lastName.setText((String) values.get("last name"));
address.setText((String) values.get("address"));
city.setText((String) values.get("city"));
state.setText((String) values.get("state"));
zip.setText((String) values.get("zip"));
phone.setText((String) values.get("phone"));
```

This is a simple but very powerful and effective way to provide a nice experience for users interacting with our system.

Sortable Tables

Tables are probably the most common way to display business data in an application. They are well known to all users and provide a universal way to view data. This has traditionally been hard to on a web page. GWT provides us with the ability to easily and quickly provide this functionality in our applications. We are going to create an application that contains a table whose rows can be sorted in an ascending or descending order by clicking on a column header. This provides for a much better user experience, as the user can modify the order of the displayed data to suit their needs. The table widgets provided with GWT does not have a built-in way to provide this capability, but GWT provides us with enough tools to add support for this easily to a table. Please keep in mind that this is just one way to create tables that can be sorted using GWT.

Time for Action—Sorting Table Rows

We do not need to create a service for this application as the sorting of data takes place on the client. We will create an application with some seed data for our table, and then add support for sorting that data by clicking on the column headers.

1. Create a new Java file named `SortableTablesPanel.java` in the `com.packtpub.gwtbook.samples.client.panels` package. We will add support to this class to make the included table sortable by clicking on the column headers. First create a `CustomerData` class that will represent one row in the table, and accessors for each field.

```java
private class CustomerData
{
  private String firstName;
  private String lastName;
  private String country;
  private String city;
  public CustomerData(String firstName, String lastName,
                                  String city, String country)
  {
    this.firstName = firstName;
    this.lastName = lastName;
    this.country = country;
    this.city = city;
  }
  public String getCountry()
  {
    return country;
  }
  public String getCity()
  {
    return city;
  }
  public String getFirstName()
  {
    return firstName;
  }
  public String getLastName()
  {
    return lastName;
  }
}
```

2. Create an `ArrayList` named `customerData` for storing the customer data. Create variables for storing the sort direction, the headers for the columns in the table, temporary data structures for sorting, and a `FlexTable` for displaying the customer data.

```
private int sortDirection = 0;
private FlexTable sortableTable = new FlexTable();
private String[] columnHeaders = new String[]
            { "First Name", "Last Name", "City", "Country" };
private ArrayList customerData = new ArrayList();
private HashMap dataBucket = new HashMap();
private ArrayList sortColumnValues = new ArrayList();
```

3. In the constructor for the `SortableTablesPanel`, create a new `VerticalPanel` that we will use as the container for the widgets that we are adding to the user interface. Set the styles for the table and set the column headers for the table.

```
VerticalPanel workPanel = new VerticalPanel();
sortableTable.setWidth(500 + "px");
sortableTable.setStyleName("sortableTable");
sortableTable.setBorderWidth(1);
sortableTable.setCellPadding(4);
sortableTable.setCellSpacing(1);
sortableTable.setHTML(0, 0, columnHeaders[0]
        + " <img border='0' src='images/blank.gif'/>");
sortableTable.setHTML(0, 1, columnHeaders[1]
        + " <img border='0' src='images/blank.gif'/>");
sortableTable.setHTML(0, 2, columnHeaders[2]
        + " <img border='0' src='images/blank.gif'/>");
sortableTable.setHTML(0, 3, columnHeaders[3]
        + " <img border='0' src='images/blank.gif'/>");
```

4. Also in the constructor, add five customers to the `customerData` list. Add the data from this list to the table and set a listener on the table that will sort the rows when the first column is clicked. We will be displaying this list of customers in the table and then sorting the table when a column header is clicked.

```
customerData.add(new CustomerData("Rahul","Dravid","Bangalore",
                                            "India"));
customerData.add(new CustomerData("Nat", "Flintoff", "London",
                                            "England"));
customerData.add(new CustomerData("Inzamamul", "Haq", "Lahore",
                                            "Pakistan"));
customerData.add(new CustomerData("Graeme", "Smith", "Durban",
```

```
                                                   "SouthAfrica"));
        customerData.add(new CustomerData("Ricky", "Ponting", "Sydney",
                                                    "Australia"));
        int row = 1;
        for (Iterator iter = customerData.iterator(); iter.hasNext();)
        {
          CustomerData element = (CustomerData) iter.next();
          sortableTable.setText(row, 0, element.getFirstName());
          sortableTable.setText(row, 1, element.getLastName());
          sortableTable.setText(row, 2, element.getCity());
          sortableTable.setText(row, 3, element.getCountry());
          row++;
        }
        RowFormatter rowFormatter = sortableTable.getRowFormatter();
        rowFormatter.setStyleName(0, "tableHeader");
        sortableTable.addTableListener(new TableListener()
        {
          public void onCellClicked(SourcesTableEvents sender, int row,
                                                          int cell)
          {
            if (row == 0)
            {
              sortTable(row, cell);
            }
          }
        });
```

5. Finally, in the constructor, add the table to the work panel. Create a little info panel that displays descriptive text about this application, so that we can display this text when this sample is selected in the list of available samples in our Samples application. Add the info panel and the work panel to a dock panel, and initialize the widget.

```
        HorizontalPanel infoPanel = new HorizontalPanel();
        infoPanel.add(new HTML(
                     "<div class='infoProse'>This example shows
                     how to create tables whose rows can be
                     sorted by clicking on the column
                     header.</div>"));
        workPanel.setStyleName("sortableTables-Panel");
        workPanel.add(sortableTable);
        DockPanel workPane = new DockPanel();
        workPane.add(infoPanel, DockPanel.NORTH);
        workPane.add(workPanel, DockPanel.CENTER);
        workPane.setCellHeight(workPanel, "100%");
```

```
workPane.setCellWidth(workPanel, "100%");
sortTable(0, 0);
initWidget(workPane);
```

5. Add a private method for redrawing the headers of the table. This is a nice way for us to redraw the table column header so that we can change the image displayed in the header to match the current sort direction.

```
private void redrawColumnHeaders(int column)
{
  if (sortDirection == 0)
  {
    sortableTable.setHTML(0, column, columnHeaders[column]
          + " <img border='0' src='images/desc.gif'/>");
  }
  else if (sortDirection == 1)
  {
    sortableTable.setHTML(0, column, columnHeaders[column]
          + " <img border='0' src='images/asc.gif'/>");
  }
  else
  {
  sortableTable.setHTML(0, column, columnHeaders[column]
          + " <img border='0' src='images/blank.gif'/>");
  }
  for (int i = 0; i < 4; i++)
  {
  if (i != column)
  {
    sortableTable.setHTML(0, i, columnHeaders[i]
          + " <img border='0' src='images/blank.gif'/>");
  }
  }
}
```

6. Add a private method to redraw the entire table when we change the sort order.

```
private void redrawTable()
{
  int row = 1;
  for (Iterator iter = sortColumnValues.iterator();
                                    iter.hasNext();)
  {
    String key = (String) iter.next();
    CustomerData custData = (CustomerData) dataBucket.get(key);
```

```
                    sortableTable.setText(row, 0, custData.getFirstName());
                    sortableTable.setText(row, 1, custData.getLastName());
                    sortableTable.setText(row, 2, custData.getCity());
                    sortableTable.setText(row, 3, custData.getCountry());
                    row++;
                }
            }
```

7. Add a private method that can sort the data in an ascending or descending way and redraw the table with the sorted rows. We are using the sort method provided by the `Collections` class to sort the data, but can also modify this to use the `Comparator` class to compare two pieces of data, and then use that for sorting.

```
        public void sortTable(int row, int cell)
        {
            dataBucket.clear();
            sortColumnValues.clear();
            for (int i = 1; i < customerData.size() + 1; i++)
            {
                dataBucket.put(sortableTable.getText(i, cell), new
                CustomerData(
                sortableTable.getText(i, 0), sortableTable.getText(i, 1),
                sortableTable.getText(i, 2), sortableTable.getText
                                                            (i, 3)));
                sortColumnValues.add(sortableTable.getText(i, cell));
            }
            if (sortDirection == 0)
            {
                sortDirection = 1;
                Collections.sort(sortColumnValues);
            }
            else
            {
                sortDirection = 0;
                Collections.reverse(sortColumnValues);
            }
            redrawColumnHeader(cell);
            resetColumnHeaders(cell);
            redrawTable();
        }
```

Here is a screenshot of the application. You can click on any of the column headers to sort the data.

Sort Tables by clicking on a column header

This example shows how to create tables whose rows can be sorted by clicking on the column header.

First Name ▲	Last Name	City	Country
Graeme	Smith	Durban	SouthAfrica
Inzamamul	Haq	Lahore	Pakistan
Nat	Flintoff	London	England
Rahul	Dravid	Bangalore	India
Ricky	Ponting	Sydney	Australia

What Just Happened?

We create a `CustomerData` class to represent each row in a `FlexTable`. We then create some customer data and store it in an `ArrayList`.

```
customerData.add(new CustomerData("Rahul", "Dravid", "Bangalore",
                                                    "India"));
```

Data from this list is added to the table. We need to specify the row number and column number in order to add an element to the table.

```
CustomerData element = (CustomerData) iter.next();
sortableTable.setText(row, 0, element.getFirstName());
sortableTable.setText(row, 1, element.getLastName());
sortableTable.setText(row, 2, element.getCity());
sortableTable.setText(row, 3, element.getCountry());
```

The column headers are contained in row zero and the table data starts from row 1. We add the column header by setting the HTML for that particular cell like this:

```
sortableTable.setHTML(0, 0, columnHeaders[0] + " 
<img border='0' src='images/blank.gif'/>");
```

This enables us to add a snippet of HTML to the cell instead of setting just plain text. We add the text for the column header along with an `img` tag with a blank image file. A column header without an image next to the text visually indicates to the user that there is no sort order specified for that particular column. When we click on a column header, we will be modifying this image to use either an ascending or descending icon. An event handler is registered to listen for clicks on the table. GWT does not contain a mechanism to register a handler when someone clicks on a specific cell, so we use the general table click listener and check to see if the click was on row zero, which is the row that contains the column headers. If the user did click on the column header, we go ahead and sort the table.

The real magic happens in the `sortTable()` method. A temporary `HashMap` named `dataBucket` is created to store the rows from the table, with each row keyed by the value in the column whose header was clicked, along with a temporary `ArrayList` named `sortColumnValues` that stores the column values in the column whose header was clicked. This means that the `sortColumnValues` list contains values that are keys in the `dataBucket` map.

```
for (int i = 1; i < customerData.size() + 1; i++)
{
  dataBucket.put(sortableTable.getText(i, cell), new CustomerData(
          sortableTable.getText(i, 0), sortableTable.getText(i, 1),
          sortableTable.getText(i, 2), sortableTable.getText(i, 3)));
          sortColumnValues.add(sortableTable.getText(i, cell));
}
```

We check the value of the `sortDirection` variable and, based on the value, sort the `sortColumnValues` list either ascending or descending to contain the column values in the right order. The built-in `sort()` and `reverseSort()` methods of the `Collections` class are used to provide the sorting mechanism.

```
if (sortDirection == 0)
{
  sortDirection = 1;
  Collections.sort(sortColumnValues);
}
else
{
  sortDirection = 0;
  Collections.reverse(sortColumnValues);
}
```

The table column headers are then redrawn so that the column that was clicked will have the right icon for the sort order and all the other column headers have only plain text and a blank image. Finally, we redraw the table by iterating through the `sortColumnValues` list and retrieving the associated `CustomerData` object from the `dataBucket` and adding it as a row in the table.

This application demonstrates the tremendous power that is provided by the GWT framework that enables you to manipulate tables to extend their functionality. GWT provides different kinds of tables for building user interfaces:

- **FlexTable**: A table that creates cells on demand. You can even have rows that contain a different number of cells. This table expands as needed when you add rows and columns to it.

- **Grid**: A table that can contain text, HTML, or child widgets. It must, however, be created explicitly with the number of desired rows and columns.

We will be using both of these table widgets extensively in the applications that we build in this chapter and the rest of this book.

Dynamic Lists

We will create an application that uses dynamic lists to present the user with a way to filter criteria for a search. In this section we are going to create dynamic tables, which will enable us to populate child tables as items in a master table are selected. We are going to do this by using GWT's AJAX support and display only those items in a child table that are relevant to the selection in the main table. This application will make it easy to navigate and filter out criteria for a search. In this sample application, we are going to enable a user to select a manufacturer of automobiles, which will automatically fill a second list with all the brands of cars made by that manufacturer. When the customer further selects an item in this list of brands, a third list will be automatically populated with the models of cars for the selected brand. In this way, a user can interactively select and navigate through the search criteria, in a user-friendly and intuitive way without having to submit data and refresh the page to present some of this information.

Time for Action—Filtering Search Criteria

As a part of this application, we will also create a service that will provide information on the manufacturers, brands, and models, and create a user interface that asynchronously retrieves this information from the service to display it to the user.

1. Create a new Java file named `DynamicListsService.java` in the `com.packtpub.gwtbook.samples.client` package. Define a `DynamicListsService` interface with methods for retrieving information about the manufacturers, brands, and models:

    ```
    public interface DynamicListsService extends RemoteService
    {
      public List getManufacturers();
      public List getBrands(String manufacturer);
      public List getModels(String manufacturer, String brand);
    }
    ```

2. Create a new Java file named `DynamicListsServiceAsync.java` in the `com.packtpub.gwtbook.samples.client` package. Define a `DynamicListsServiceAsync` interface:

    ```
    public interface DynamicListsServiceAsync
    {
      public void getManufacturers(AsyncCallback callback);
      public void getBrands(String manufacturer,
                                       AsyncCallback callback);
      public void getModels(String manufacturer, String brand,
                                       AsyncCallback callback);
    }
    ```

3. Create a new Java file named `DynamicListsServiceImpl.java` in the `com.packtpub.gwtbook.samples.server` package. Define a `DynamicListsServiceImpl` class that extends `RemoteServiceServlet` and implements the previously created `DynamicListsService` interface. This class will return information about the manufacturers, brands, and models. Create a class named `Manufacturer` to encapsulate the information about each manufacturer, including the brands and models of automobiles offered by them.

    ```
    private class Manufacturer
    {
      private HashMap brands = new HashMap();
      public Manufacturer(HashMap brands)
      {
        this.brands = brands;
    ```

```
    }
    public HashMap getBrands()
    {
      return brands;
    }
  }
```

4. Create a private method to load the manufacturer information into a
   HashMap. The data on the manufacturers will be loaded into the first table
   later on. When the user interface starts up, the manufacturers table is the only
   one with the data, and provides the starting point for using the application.

```
private void loadData()
{
  ArrayList brandModels = new ArrayList();
  brandModels.add("EX");
  brandModels.add("DX Hatchback");
  brandModels.add("DX 4-Door");
  HashMap manufacturerBrands = new HashMap();
  manufacturerBrands.put("Civic", brandModels);
  brandModels = new ArrayList();
  brandModels.add("SX");
  brandModels.add("Sedan");
  manufacturerBrands.put("Accord", brandModels);
  brandModels = new ArrayList();
  brandModels.add("LX");
  brandModels.add("Deluxe");
  manufacturerBrands.put("Odyssey", brandModels);
  Manufacturer manufacturer = new
                              Manufacturer(manufacturerBrands);
  data.put("Honda", manufacturer);
  brandModels = new ArrayList();
  brandModels.add("LXE");
  brandModels.add("LX");
  manufacturerBrands = new HashMap();
  manufacturerBrands.put("Altima", brandModels);
  brandModels = new ArrayList();
  brandModels.add("NX");
  brandModels.add("EXE");
  manufacturerBrands.put("Sentra", brandModels);
  manufacturer = new Manufacturer(manufacturerBrands);
  data.put("Nissan", manufacturer);
  brandModels = new ArrayList();
  brandModels.add("E300");
  brandModels.add("E500");
```

```
        manufacturerBrands = new HashMap();
        manufacturerBrands.put("E-Class", brandModels);
        brandModels = new ArrayList();
        brandModels.add("C250");
        brandModels.add("C300");
        manufacturerBrands.put("C-Class", brandModels);
        manufacturer = new Manufacturer(manufacturerBrands);
        data.put("Mercedes", manufacturer);
    }
```

5. Implement the service method for retrieving a list of manufacturers.

```
    public ArrayList getManufacturers()
    {
      ArrayList manufacturersList = new ArrayList();
      for (Iterator iter=data.keySet().iterator(); iter.hasNext();)
      {
        manufacturersList.add((String) iter.next());
      }
      return manufacturersList;
    }
```

6. Implement the service method for retrieving the list of brands offered by a manufacturer.

```
    public ArrayList getBrands(String manufacturer)
    {
      ArrayList brandsList = new ArrayList();
      for (Iterator iter = ((Manufacturer)data.get(manufacturer))
                 .getBrands().keySet().iterator(); iter.hasNext();)
      {
        brandsList.add((String) iter.next());
      }
      return brandsList;
    }
```

7. Implement the service method for retrieving the models offered by a manufacturer for a particular brand.

```
    public ArrayList getModels(String manufacturer, String brand)
    {
      ArrayList modelsList = new ArrayList();
      Manufacturer mfr = (Manufacturer) data.get(manufacturer);
      HashMap mfrBrands = (HashMap) mfr.getBrands();
      for (Iterator iter = ((ArrayList)
              mfrBrands.get(brand)).iterator();  iter.hasNext();)
      {
```

```
          modelsList.add((String) iter.next());
      }
      return modelsList;
  }
```

8. Create the user interface for this application in a new Java file named
   DynamicListsPanel.java in the com.packtpub.gwtbook.samples.
   client.panels package. Create three Grid widgets to hold the
   manufacturers, brands, and models information and add them to the main
   panel. Create the service class that we are going to invoke.

```
Grid manufacturers = new Grid(5, 1);
Grid brands = new Grid(5, 1);
Grid models = new Grid(5, 1);
final DynamicListsServiceAsync dynamicListsService =
(DynamicListsServiceAsync) GWT.create
                             (DynamicListsService.class);
```

9. Add a private method for clearing out the panels.

```
public void clearSelections(Grid grid, boolean clearData)
{
  for (int i = 0; i < grid.getRowCount(); i++)
  {
    if (clearData)
    {
      grid.setText(i, 0, " ");
    }
  }
}
```

10. In the constructor for the DynamicListsPanel, create a new
    HorizontalPanel that we will use as the container for the widgets that we
    are adding to the user interface. Also, create the service target and set its
    entry point.

```
HorizontalPanel workPanel = new HorizontalPanel();
ServiceDefTarget endpoint = (ServiceDefTarget)
                                        dynamicListsService;
endpoint.setServiceEntryPoint("/Samples/dynamiclists");
```

11. In the same constructor, add an event handler to listen for clicks on the Select
    Manufacturer table.

```
manufacturers.addTableListener(new TableListener()
                    {
                    public void onCellClicked
                            (SourcesTableEvents sender,
                                    int row, int cell)
```

```
                                 {
                                  clearSelections(manufacturers,
                                                         false);
                                  clearSelections(brands, true);
                                  clearSelections(models, true);
                                  selectedManufacturer = row;
                                  AsyncCallback callback = new
                                                  AsyncCallback()
                                  {
                                    public void onSuccess(Object
                                                            result)
                                    {
                                      brands.clear();
                                      int row = 0;
                                      for (Iterator iter =
                                              ((ArrayList) result).
                                                        iterator();
                                      iter.hasNext();)
                                        {
                                          brands.setText(row++, 0,
                                               (String) iter.next());
                                        }
                                    }
                                    public void onFailure(Throwable
                                                            caught)
                                    {
                                      Window.alert("Error calling
                                      the Dynamic Lists service to
                                      get the brands." +
                                              caught.getMessage());
                                    }
                                  };
                                  dynamicListsService.getBrands
                                  (manufacturers.getText(row,
                                              cell),callback);
                                }
                              });
```

12. In the same constructor, add an event handler to listen for clicks on the Select
    Brand table.

```
brands.addTableListener
   (new TableListener()
                     {
                      public void onCellClicked
                      (SourcesTableEvents sender, int row, int cell)
```

```
                    {
                      clearSelections(brands, false);
                      clearSelections(models, true);
                      AsyncCallback callback = new
                                                AsyncCallback()
                    {
                      public void onSuccess(Object result)
                      {
                        models.clear();
                        int row = 0;
                        for (Iterator iter = ((ArrayList)
                         result).iterator(); iter.hasNext();)
                        {
                          models.setText(row++, 0, (String)
                                                iter.next());
                        }
                      }
                      public void onFailure(Throwable caught)
                      {
                      Window.alert("Error calling the Dynamic
                      Lists service to get the models." +
                                        caught.getMessage());
                      }
                    };
                    dynamicListsService.getModels
                      (manufacturers.getText
                      (selectedManufacturer, cell),
                      brands.getText(row, cell), callback);
                }
            });
```

13. Also in the constructor, add a listener to the Select Models table to clear out the selections when a model is selected. Load the Select Manufacturer table with data when the application starts.

```
models.addTableListener(new TableListener()
                {
                    public void onCellClicked
                        (SourcesTableEvents sender, int row,
                                                int cell)
                    {
                      clearSelections(models, false);
                      models.getCellFormatter()
                      .setStyleName(row, cell,
                                "dynamicLists-Selected");
```

```
                              }
                          });
        AsyncCallback callback = new AsyncCallback()
        {
          public void onSuccess(Object result)
          {
            int row = 0;
            for (Iterator iter = ((ArrayList) result).iterator();
                                         iter.hasNext();)
            {
              manufacturers.setText(row++, 0, (String) iter.next());
            }
          }
          public void onFailure(Throwable caught)
          {
            Window.alert("Error calling the Dynamic Lists service to
                       get the manufacturers." + caught.getMessage());
          }
        };
        dynamicListsService.getManufacturers(callback);
```

14. In the constructor, create a VerticalPanel named itemPanel, and add each table and its associated label to it. Create an itemPanel for each of the three tables, set the style, and add them to the workPanel.

```
        VerticalPanel itemPanel = new VerticalPanel();
        Label itemLabel = new Label("Select Manufacturer");
        itemLabel.setStyleName("dynamicLists-Label");
        itemPanel.add(itemLabel);
        itemPanel.add(manufacturers);
        workPanel.add(itemPanel);
        itemPanel = new VerticalPanel();
        itemLabel = new Label("Select Brand");
        itemLabel.setStyleName("dynamicLists-Label");
        itemPanel.add(itemLabel);
        itemPanel.add(brands);
        workPanel.add(itemPanel);
        itemPanel = new VerticalPanel();
        itemLabel = new Label("Models");
        itemLabel.setStyleName("dynamicLists-Label");
        itemPanel.add(itemLabel);
        itemPanel.add(models);
        workPanel.add(itemPanel);
        manufacturers.setStyleName("dynamicLists-List");
```

```
brands.setStyleName("dynamicLists-List");
models.setStyleName("dynamicLists-List");
workPanel.setStyleName("dynamicLists-Panel");
```

15. Finally, in the constructor, create a little info panel that displays descriptive text about this application, so that we can display this text when this sample is selected in the list of available samples in our `Samples` application. Add the info panel and the work panel to a dock panel, and set the widget.

```
HorizontalPanel infoPanel = new HorizontalPanel();
infoPanel.add(new HTML(
                  "<div class='infoProse'>This example
                  demonstrates the creation of dynamic
                  lists. You select an item from the first
                  list and corresponding items are retrieved
                  asynchronously from the server to display
                  in the second list. You can then select an
                  item in the second list to get another
                  selection of items. In this particular
                  example, we retrieve car brand by
                  manufacturer, and then get and display the
                  specific models for the selected
                  brand.</div>"));
DockPanel workPane = new DockPanel();
workPane.add(infoPanel, DockPanel.NORTH);
workPane.add(workPanel, DockPanel.CENTER);
workPane.setCellHeight(workPanel, "100%");
workPane.setCellWidth(workPanel, "100%");
initWidget(workPane);
```

16. Add the service to the module file for the `Samples` application—`Samples. gwt.xml` in the `com.packtpub.gwtbook.samples` package.

```
<servlet path="/dynamiclists" class=
"com.packtpub.gwtbook.samples.server.DynamicListsServiceImpl"/>
```

Here is a screenshot of the application when we have selected one of the manufacturers—Mercedes, and one of its brands—E-class:

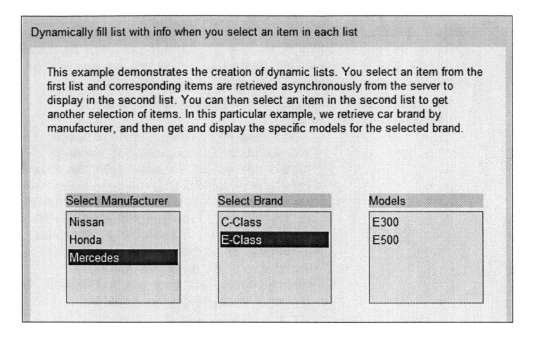

What Just Happened?

We create a list of the Manufacturer objects, one per manufacturer. Each of these Manufacturer objects contains a HashMap named brands, which contains an ArrayList of models for that particular brand. This data structure that we have just created contains all the information we need regarding the brands and models offered by a manufacturer. In an actual application this data would usually be retrieved from an enterprise data source. For instance, here is how we build up the data for the manufacturer Mercedes:

```
brandModels = new ArrayList();
brandModels.add("E300");
brandModels.add("E500");
manufacturerBrands = new HashMap();
manufacturerBrands.put("E-Class", brandModels);
brandModels = new ArrayList();
brandModels.add("C250");
brandModels.add("C300");
manufacturerBrands.put("C-Class", brandModels);
manufacturer = new Manufacturer(manufacturerBrands);
data.put("Mercedes", manufacturer);
```

We then implement the three service methods from the interface to return a list of manufacturers, a list of brands for a given manufacturer, and finally a list of models for a given manufacturer and brand. Each of these methods navigates the Manufacturer objects, and retrieves and returns a list with the necessary information. When we request a list of models for a given brand and manufacturer, the service method implementation returns the list by navigating the manufacturers list like this:

```
Manufacturer mfr = (Manufacturer) data.get(manufacturer);
HashMap mfrBrands = (HashMap) mfr.getBrands();
for (Iterator iter = ((ArrayList) mfrBrands.get(brand)).iterator();
                                                 iter.hasNext();)
{
  modelsList.add((String) iter.next());
}
return modelsList;
```

The user interface consists of three Grid widgets. A Grid is another kind of a table widget that can contain text, HTML, or a child widget within its cells. When the application is initialized, the list of manufacturers is initially retrieved from the DynamicListsService and the manufacturers grid is filled with the data. An event handler is registered to listen for clicks in the grids. When an item in the manufacturers grid is clicked, we clear the brands grid first and then invoke the getBrands() method on the service and load the brands grid with the retrieved information. When the user selects an item from the brands grid by clicking on it, we first clear the models grid and then we invoke the getModels() method on the service and load the models grid with the retrieved information. Every time we make a selection in any of the grids, we were able to retrieve all this information using GWT without any page refreshes or page submissions!

Flickr-Style Editable Labels

Flickr (http://flickr.com/) is one of the most innovative Web 2.0 sites on the Internet. Its use of AJAX makes this website a pleasure to use. A prime example of this is the label widget that is displayed below any image that you add to your flickr account. It looks like a simple label, but when you hover the cursor over it, it changes color indicating that it is more than a label. When you click on it, it transforms into a text box where you can edit the text in the label! You even get buttons to make your changes persist or cancel to discard your changes. After you save or cancel, it transforms back into a label again. Try it out. It is really neat! This is a great way of combining multiple HTML controls—a label, text box, and buttons into one compound control that saves valuable space on the web page, while providing the necessary functionality in a very user-friendly manner. In this section, we are going to recreate the flickr-style label using the widgets available to us in GWT.

Time for Action—A Custom Editable Label

We are going to create a label that is dynamically converted into an editable text box when you click on it. It will also provide you with the ability to save changes or discard changes. If you modify the text and save the changes, the label text will be changed, otherwise the original text will be retained, and the text box will be transformed back into a label. It is a very innovative user interface and you really need to use it to appreciate it!

1. Create a new Java file named `FlickrEditableLabelPanel.java` in the `com.packtpub.gwtbook.samples.client.panels` package. Create an image, a label, a text box and two buttons for the user interface.

    ```java
    private Label originalName;
    private String originalText;
    private Button saveButton;
    private Button cancelButton;
    private Image image = new Image("images/sample.jpg");
    private Label orLabel = new Label("or");
    ```

2. Create a private method for displaying the text box along with the buttons while hiding the label. This is what will essentially transform the label into a text box with buttons!

    ```java
    private void ShowText()
    {
      originalText = originalName.getText();
      originalName.setVisible(false);
      saveButton.setVisible(true);
      orLabel.setVisible(true);
      cancelButton.setVisible(true);
      newName.setText(originalText);
      newName.setVisible(true);
      newName.setFocus(true);
      newName.setStyleName("flickrPanel-textBox-edit");
    }
    ```

3. In the constructor for `FlickrEditableLabelPanel`, create an event handler that listens for a click on the label, and invokes the above method.

    ```java
    originalName.addClickListener(new ClickListener()
    {
      public void onClick(Widget sender)
      {
        ShowText();
      }
    });
    ```

4. Also, in the constructor, create an event handler that listens for a mouse hover and modifies the label style to provide a visual cue to the user to click on the label.

```
originalName.addMouseListener(new MouseListener()
                         {
                           public void onMouseDown
                               (Widget sender, int x, int y)
                           {
                           }
                           public void onMouseEnter
                                           (Widget sender)
                           {
                             originalName.setStyleName
                                 "flickrPanel-label-hover");
                           }
                           public void onMouseLeave
                                           (Widget sender)
                           {
                             originalName.setStyleName
                                     ("flickrPanel-label");
                           }
                           public void onMouseMove
                               (Widget sender, int x, int y)
                           {
                           }
                           public void onMouseUp
                               (Widget sender, int x, int y)
                           {
                           }
                         });
```

5. Create a text box for typing in the new name in the constructor and create an event handler that listens for the return key and escape key when the focus is in the text box, and either saves the change or cancels out.

```
newName.addKeyboardListener(new KeyboardListenerAdapter()
                         {
                           public void onKeyPress(Widget
                           sender, char keyCode, int
                                             modifiers)
                           {
                             switch (keyCode)
                             {
                               case KeyboardListenerAdapter.
                                   KEY_ENTER:saveChange();
                               break;
```

```
                                    case KeyboardListenerAdapter.
                                        KEY_ESCAPE:cancelChange();
                                    break;
                                }
                            }
                        });
```

6. Create an event handler in the constructor to listen for a click on the save button and save the changes.

```
saveButton.addClickListener(new ClickListener()
                        {
                            public void onClick(Widget sender)
                            {
                                saveChange();
                            }
                        });
```

7. Create an event handler in the constructor to listen for a click on the cancel button and discard any changes made.

```
cancelButton.addClickListener(new ClickListener()
                        {
                            public void onClick(Widget sender)
                            {
                                cancelChange();
                            }
                        });
```

8. In the constructor, set the visibility of the widgets when the application is first loaded. When the user interface is first displayed, we want the label to be shown and everything else hidden.

```
originalName.setVisible(true);
newName.setVisible(false);
saveButton.setVisible(false);
orLabel.setVisible(false);
cancelButton.setVisible(false);
```

9. Finally, in the constructor, create a `HorizontalPanel` named `buttonPanel` and add the widgets that we created to it. Create a `VerticalPanel` named `workPanel` and add the `buttonPanel` to it. Create a little info panel that displays descriptive text about this application, so that we can display this text when this sample is selected in the list of available samples in our `Samples` application. Add the info panel and the work panel to a dock panel, and initialize the widget.

```
HorizontalPanel buttonPanel = new HorizontalPanel();
buttonPanel.setStyleName("flickrPanel-buttonPanel");
buttonPanel.add(saveButton);
buttonPanel.add(orLabel);
buttonPanel.add(cancelButton);
DockPanel workPane = new DockPanel();
workPane.add(infoPanel, DockPanel.NORTH);
VerticalPanel workPanel = new VerticalPanel();
workPanel.setStyleName("flickrPanel");
workPanel.add(image);
workPanel.add(originalName);
workPanel.add(newName);
workPanel.add(buttonPanel);
workPane.add(workPanel, DockPanel.CENTER);
workPane.setCellHeight(workPanel, "100%");
workPane.setCellWidth(workPanel, "100%");
initWidget(workPane);
```

10. Create a private method for displaying the label and hiding the text. Now we are hiding the label and displaying our nice text-editing interface with the text box and the buttons for saving or discarding changes made.

```
private void showLabel()
{
  originalName.setVisible(true);
  saveButton.setVisible(false);
  orLabel.setVisible(false);
  cancelButton.setVisible(false);
  newName.setVisible(false);
}
```

11. Create a private method for saving the changes.

```
private void saveChange()
{
  originalName.setText(newName.getText());
  showLabel();
   // This is where you can call an RPC service to update
   // a db or call some other service to propagate
   // the change. In this example we just change the
   // text of the label.
}
```

12. Create a method for discarding the changes.

```
public void cancelChange()
{
  originalName.setText(originalText);
  showLabel();
}
```

This is what the application looks like when you visit the page:

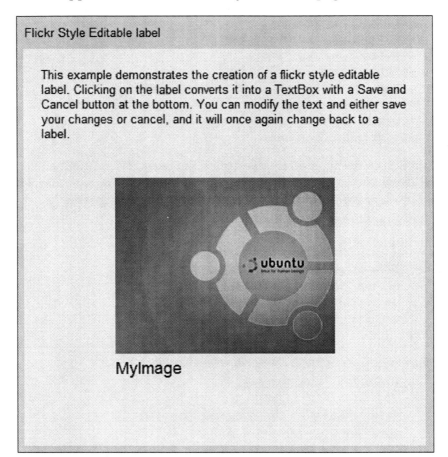

If you click on the label under the image, it will be converted to a text box with a save and cancel button. You can modify the text and save changes or click on cancel to change back to a label.

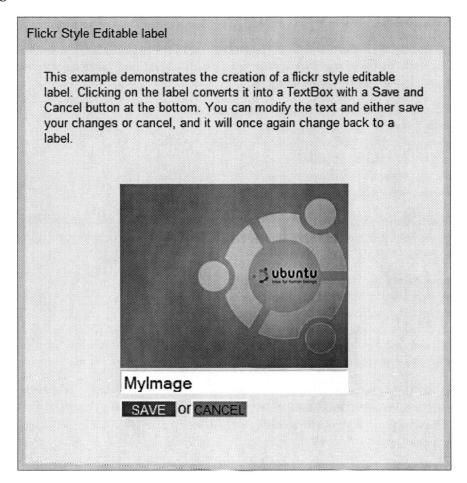

What Just Happened?

We create an user interface that consists of an image with a label under it, a text box, a save button, a label, and a cancel button. An event handler is registered to listen for clicks on the label. When the user clicks on the label, the event handler is triggered, and we hide the label, and set the text box and the buttons to be visible.

```
originalText = originalName.getText();
originalName.setVisible(false);
saveButton.setVisible(true);
orLabel.setVisible(true);
```

```
cancelButton.setVisible(true);
newName.setText(originalText);
newName.setVisible(true);
newName.setFocus(true);
newName.setStyleName("flickrPanel-textBox-edit");
```

If we modify the text and click save, the event handler that is listening for the click on the save button saves the text as the values of the label and once again displays the label and hides all the other widgets.

```
originalName.setText(newName.getText());
originalName.setVisible(true);
saveButton.setVisible(false);
orLabel.setVisible(false);
cancelButton.setVisible(false);
newName.setVisible(false);
```

If we discard the changes by clicking the cancel button, the event handler that is listening for the click on the cancel button will display the label and hide all the other widgets.

```
originalName.setText(originalText);
originalName.setVisible(true);
saveButton.setVisible(false);
orLabel.setVisible(false);
cancelButton.setVisible(false);
newName.setVisible(false);
```

In this application we do not invoke any services to propagate the change to a server-side process, but we can easily do that by adding the code to invoke a service when we save the change made to the text.

Summary

In this chapter we took a look at creating a live search application. Then we took a look at creating a password strength checker. Also, we created forms that can be auto-filled with information from the server. We also created applications where tables were sorted. Then before creating a flickr-style editable label, we created dynamically populating lists based on user selection.

In the next chapter, we are going to look at creating responsive complex interfaces, which use some of the more advanced features of GWT.

5
Responsive Complex Interfaces

In this chapter, we will create user interfaces that demonstrate some advanced features of GWT.

The tasks that we will address are:

- Pageable tables
- Editable tree nodes
- Log spy
- Sticky notes
- Jigsaw puzzle

Pageable Tables

We are going to start exploring more complex GWT user interfaces in this chapter. We routinely come across some cases in today's business world where we need to use tables to display a large amount of data. Displaying all of the available data in a table at once is not a viable option, either from the point of view of usability or from a practical perspective.

We can also potentially lock up the browser that is displaying the table, if the dataset retrieved is of a large enough size. A much better way to display this data to users would be to show them a fixed number of results first, and then provide them with the mechanism to navigate through the results; so that they can page back and forward through the data at their leisure. This makes for a nicer user experience, and also loads the smaller dataset much faster.

In this section, we are going to create an application that provides this functionality. As a part of this sample, we are also going to learn how to use an embedded database with a GWT application.

Time for Action—Interfacing a Dataset

We will create an application that will let us retrieve data in chunks or pages, instead of getting everything at once. We will do this by retrieving the first ten items as a result of a query, and provide a way for the user to either go forward or backward through this set of results. The steps are as follows:

1. Create a new Java file named `PageableDataService.java` in the `com.packtpub.gwtbook.samples.client` package. Define the `PageableDataService` interface with one method to retrieve the customer data, by providing a start index and the number of items to retrieve as parameters:

    ```
    public interface PageableDataService extends RemoteService
    {
        public List getCustomerData(int startIndex, int numItems );
    }
    ```

2. Create the asynchronous version of this service definition interface in a new Java file named `PageableDataServiceAsync.java` in the `com.packtpub.gwtbook.samples.client` package:

    ```
    public interface PageableDataServiceAsync
    {
        public void getCustomerData(int startIndex, int numItems,
        AsyncCallback callback);
    }
    ```

3. Create the implementation of our pageable data service in a new Java file named `PageableDataServiceImpl.java` in the `com.packtpub.gwtbook.samples.server` package. Create a private `ArrayList` object named `customerData` that will be the container for the customer data:

    ```
    private ArrayList customerData = new ArrayList();
    ```

4. It will be simpler if we use a database for storing our data instead of managing data structures in our service. We are going to use HSQLDB—a small embedded database for storing the data that we will be accessing in this service. First, load the data from the pre-populated database into a list:

```
private void loadData()
{
  Class.forName("org.hsqldb.jdbcDriver");
  Connection conn = DriverManager.getConnection
  ( "jdbc:hsqldb:file:samplesdb", "sa", "");
  Statement st = conn.createStatement();
  ResultSet rs = st.executeQuery("SELECT * FROM users");
  for (; rs.next();)
  {
    ArrayList customer = new ArrayList();
    customer.add((String) rs.getObject(2));
    customer.add((String) rs.getObject(3));
    customer.add((String) rs.getObject(4));
    customer.add((String) rs.getObject(5));
    customer.add((String) rs.getObject(6));
    customerData.add(customer);
  }
  st.execute("SHUTDOWN");
  conn.close();
}
```

5. We call the loadData() function in the constructor for the service, so that all the required data is loaded and is available after the service is initialized:

```
public PageableDataServiceImpl()
{
  super();
  loadData();
}
```

6. Now add the service-implementation method that will send back only the requested subset of the data:

```
public ArrayList getCustomerData(int startIndex, int numItems)
{
  ArrayList customers = new ArrayList();
  for (int i = startIndex - 1; i < (startIndex + numItems); i++)
  {
    customers.add((ArrayList) customerData.get(i));
  }
  return customers;
}
```

7. Now create the user interface for interacting with the pageable data service. Create a new Java file named `PageableDataPanel.java` in the `com.packtpub.gwtbook.samples.client.panels` package. As mentioned at the beginning of the previous chapter, each of the user interfaces created in this book will be added to a sample application that is similar to the `KitchenSink` application that is available as one of the sample projects with the GWT download. That is why we will create each user interface as a panel that extends the `SamplePanel` class, and we will add the created panel to the list of sample panels in the sample application. The `SamplePanel` class and the structure of our `Samples` application are discussed at the beginning of the previous chapter. Add a `FlexTable` class for displaying the data, along with buttons for paging *forward* and *backward* through the data. Create an array of strings to store the column headers, and an integer variable to store the start index into the customer data list:

```
private FlexTable customerTable = new FlexTable();
private Button backButton = new Button("<<<");
private Button forwardButton = new Button(">>>");
private String[] customerTableHeaders = new String[]
    { "Name", "City","Zip Code", "State", "Phone" };
private int startIndex = 1;
```

8. Create the service class that we will use for invoking the service to get the data:

```
final PageableDataServiceAsync pageableDataService =
(PageableDataServiceAsync)
GWT.create(PageableDataService.class);
ServiceDefTarget endpoint = (ServiceDefTarget)
pageableDataService;
endpoint.setServiceEntryPoint(GWT.getModuleBaseURL() +
                                            "pageabledata");
```

9. Add a private method for clearing out the table before we populate it with data:

```
private void clearTable()
{
  for (int row=1; row<customerTable.getRowCount(); row++)
  {
    for (int col=0; col<customerTable.getCellCount(row); col++)
    {
      customerTable.clearCell(row, col);
    }
  }
}
```

10. Add a private method for updating the table with data retrieved from the service:

```
private void update(int startIndex)
{
  AsyncCallback callback = new AsyncCallback()
  public void onSuccess(Object result)
  {
    ArrayList customerData = (ArrayList) result;
    int row = 1;
    clearTable();
    for (Iterator iter=customerData.iterator(); iter.hasNext();)
    {
      ArrayList customer = (ArrayList) iter.next();
      customerTable.setText(row, 0, (String) customer.get(0));
      customerTable.setText(row, 1, (String) customer.get(1));
      customerTable.setText(row, 2, (String) customer.get(2));
      customerTable.setText(row, 3, (String) customer.get(3));
      customerTable.setText(row, 4, (String) customer.get(4));
      row++;
    }
  }
  public void onFailure(Throwable caught)
  {
    Window.alert("Error when invoking the pageable data service
                                : " + caught.getMessage());
  }
  pageableDataService.getCustomerData(startIndex, 10, callback);
}
```

11. In the constructor for PageableDataPanel, create a VerticalPanel object that will be the container panel for this user interface, and initialize the table that will hold the customer data:

```
VerticalPanel workPanel = new VerticalPanel();
customerTable.setWidth(500 + "px");
customerTable.setBorderWidth(1);
customerTable.setCellPadding(4);
customerTable.setCellSpacing(1);
customerTable.setText(0, 0, customerTableHeaders[0]);
customerTable.setText(0, 1, customerTableHeaders[1]);
customerTable.setText(0, 2, customerTableHeaders[2]);
customerTable.setText(0, 3, customerTableHeaders[3]);
customerTable.setText(0, 4, customerTableHeaders[4]);
```

12. Create an inner navigation bar that holds the back and forward buttons:

```
HorizontalPanel innerNavBar = new HorizontalPanel();
innerNavBar.setStyleName("pageableData-NavBar");
innerNavBar.setSpacing(8);
innerNavBar.add(backButton);
innerNavBar.add(forwardButton);
```

13. Add an event handler to listen for clicks on the back button to the constructor:

```
backButton.addClickListener(new ClickListener()
                        {
                            public void onClick(Widget sender)
                            {
                                if (startIndex >= 10)
                                startIndex -= 10;
                                update(startIndex);
                            }
                        });
```

14. Add an event handler to listen for clicks on the forward button to the constructor:

```
forwardButton.addClickListener(new ClickListener()
                        {
                            public void onClick(Widget
                                                      sender)
                            {
                                if (startIndex < 40)
                                {
                                    startIndex += 10;
                                    update(startIndex);
                                }
                            }
                        });
```

15. Finally, in the constructor, add the customer data table and the navigation bar to the work panel. Create a little info panel that displays descriptive text about this application, so that we can display the text when this sample is selected in the list of available samples in our Samples application. Add the info panel and the work panel to a dock panel, and initialize the widget. Call the update() method, so that we can get the first batch of customer data and display it when the page is initially loaded:

```
workPanel.add(innerNavBar);
HorizontalPanel infoPanel = new HorizontalPanel();
infoPanel.add(new HTML("<div class='infoProse'>Create lists
        that can be paged by fetching data from the server on demand
```

```
                we go forward and backward in the list.</div>"));
workPanel.add(customerTable);
DockPanel workPane = new DockPanel();
workPane.add(infoPanel, DockPanel.NORTH);
workPane.add(workPanel, DockPanel.CENTER);
workPane.setCellHeight(workPanel, "100%");
workPane.setCellWidth(workPanel, "100%");
initWidget(workPane);
update(1);
```

16. Add the service to the module file for the `Samples` application — `Samples.gwt.xml` — in the `com.packtpub.gwtbook.samples` package:

```
<servlet path="/Samples/pageabledata" class=
"com.packtpub.gwtbook.samples.server.PageableDataServiceImpl"/>
```

Here is the user interface for the application:

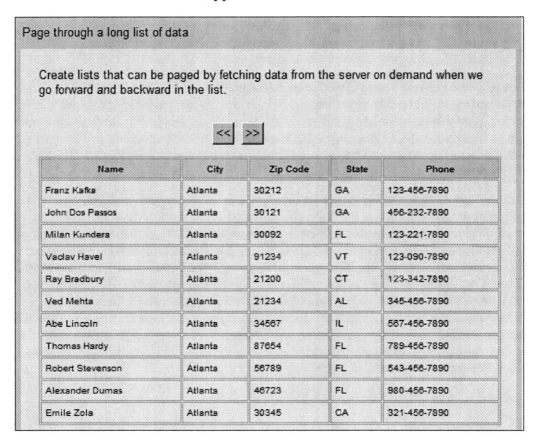

Click on the buttons to go either forward or backward in the list.

What Just Happened?

We are using an embedded database (Hypersonic SQL—HSQLDB—http://www. hsqldb.org) containing the customer data that we will page through, displaying only ten results at a time. All the components required to use this database are contained in the hsqldb.jar file. In order to use it in a GWT project, we need to ensure that the hsqldb.jar file is added to the buildpath for the Eclipse project. Then it will be available on the classpath, when you either run or debug the project.

The in-memory version of HSQLDB is being used, which means that the database runs in the same Java Virtual Machine as our GWT application. After initializing the JDBC driver for HSQLDB, we get a connection to a database named samplesdb, by specifying the database file path. If this file does not exist, it will be created, and if it does exist, the database will be loaded by the database engine. The file path provided is relative to the directory from which this JVM was started; so in our case, the database file will be created in the root directory of our project.

```
Class.forName("org.hsqldb.jdbcDriver");
Connection conn = DriverManager.getConnection
("jdbc:hsqldb:file:samplesdb", "sa", "");
```

The data from the customer table is retrieved and stored in a local ArrayList. This list data structure contains one ArrayList per row in the customers table. It will be used as the base for retrieving sets of information. Each request to retrieve customer data will provide a start index and the number of items to be retrieved. The start index tells us the offset into the ArrayList, while the number of items limits the results returned.

The user interface for the application displays a table along with two buttons. The back button pages backward through the dataset, while the forward button lets us move forward through the list. When the page is loaded, an asynchronous call is made to the PageableDataService interface to get the first ten items and display them in the table. Event handlers are registered to listen for clicks on the two buttons. Clicking on either of the buttons triggers a call to the remote service to get the next set of items. We store the start index of the currently displayed table items in a private variable. This variable is decremented when we click on the back button, and incremented when we click on the forward button. It is provided as a parameter to the remote method when we request the next set of data. The result from the request is used to populate the table on the page.

```
ArrayList customerData = (ArrayList) result;
int row = 1;
clearTable();
for (Iterator iter = customerData.iterator(); iter.hasNext();)
{
```

```
    ArrayList customer = (ArrayList) iter.next();
    customerTable.setText(row, 0, (String) customer.get(0));
    customerTable.setText(row, 1, (String) customer.get(1));
    customerTable.setText(row, 2, (String) customer.get(2));
    customerTable.setText(row, 3, (String) customer.get(3));
    customerTable.setText(row, 4, (String) customer.get(4));
    row++;
}
```

We clear out the data in the table and then add new data by setting the text for each column.

Editable Tree Nodes

Tree controls provide a very user-friendly way to display a set of hierarchical data—the common examples being the directory structure on your file system or the nodes in an XML document. GWT provides a tree widget that can display this data, but does not provide any way to modify the nodes of the tree itself. One of the most common uses of modifying a displayed node in a tree control is the renaming of files and folders in your file explorer, on your favorite platform. We are going to create an application that shows how to edit the displayed node in a tree by just clicking on it and typing in the new text. This sample also demonstrates how easy it is to extend GWT to make it do some of the things that are not provided out of the box.

Time for Action—Modifying the Node

We will create an application that contains a tree that behaves similarly to the Windows file explorer, by allowing us to click on a node and edit the text for the node. The steps are as follows:

1. Create the user interface for this application in a new Java file named EditableTreeNodesPanel.java in the com.packtpub.gwtbook.samples. client.panels package. This class also extends the SamplePanel class like all the other user interfaces in this book. A SamplePanel class extends the Composite class, and is a simple way to create several user interfaces, and add each of them to our Samples application, so that we can display a list of all the applications in a manner similar to the KitchenSink sample project from the GWT distribution. We have described the sample application structure in a section at the beginning of Chapter 4. Create a tree, a text box, and a label. Finally, create variables for the work panel and the work pane:

    ```
    private Tree editableTree = new Tree();
    private TreeItem currentSelection = new TreeItem();
    ```

```
private TextBox textbox = new TextBox();
private AbsolutePanel workPanel = new AbsolutePanel();
private DockPanel workPane = new DockPanel();
```

2. Create a private method that populates the tree with some nodes:

```
private void initTree()
{
  TreeItem root = new TreeItem("root");
  root.setState(true);
  int index = 100;
  for (int j = 0; j < 10; j++)
  {
    TreeItem item = new TreeItem();
    item.setText("File " + indcx++);
    root.addItem(item);
  }
  editableTree.addItem(root);
}
```

3. In the constructor for EditableTreeNodesPanel, initialize the tree and add an event handler for listening to clicks on the tree node:

```
initTree();
editableTree.addTreeListener(new TreeListener()
{
  public void onTreeItemSelected(TreeItem item)
  {
    if (textbox.isAttached())
    {
      if(!currentSelection.getText().equals(textbox.getText()))
      {
        currentSelection.setText(textbox.getText());
      }
      workPanel.remove(textbox);
    }
    textbox.setHeight(item.getOffsetHeight() + "px");
    textbox.setWidth("90px");
    int xpos = item.getAbsoluteLeft() - 133;
    int ypos = item.getAbsoluteTop() - 115;
    workPanel.add(textbox, xpos, ypos);
    textbox.setText(item.getText());
    textbox.setFocus(true);
    currentSelection = item;
    textbox.addFocusListener(new FocusListener()
                            {
```

```
                              public void onLostFocus(Widget
                                                        sender)
                    {
                      if (sender.isAttached())
                      {
                        if (!currentSelection.getText()
                            .equals(textbox.getText()))
                        {
                          currentSelection.setText
                                  (textbox.getText());
                        }
                        workPanel.remove(textbox);
                      }
                    }
                  });
      }
      public void onTreeItemStateChanged(TreeItem item)
      {
      }
    }
```

4. In the constructor, create a little info panel that displays descriptive text
    about this application, so that we can display the text when this sample is
    selected in the list of available samples in our `Samples` application. Add the
    info panel and the work panel to the dock panel, and initialize the widget:

```
HorizontalPanel infoPanel = new HorizontalPanel();
infoPanel.add(new HTML
  ("<div class='infoProse'>This sample shows a tree whose nodes
    can be edited by clicking on a tree node.</div>"));
workPanel.add(editableTree);
workPane.add(infoPanel, DockPanel.NORTH);
workPane.add(workPanel, DockPanel.CENTER);
workPane.setCellHeight(workPanel, "100%");
workPane.setCellWidth(workPanel, "100%");
initWidget(workPane);
```

Run the application:

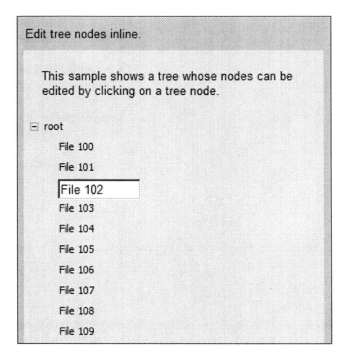

You can click on a tree node and change the text in the text box that is displayed.

What Just Happened?

Tree controls are a nice way to visualize and explore hierarchical data. In this sample, we create a tree with ten nodes, each node containing a string value. We register an event handler that listens for selection events on the tree nodes. When a tree node is selected, we create a text box that contains the same text as the tree node, and position the text box over the tree node. The text box is positioned by retrieving the left and top coordinates for the tree node. The currently selected tree node is stored in a private variable. An event handler is registered to listen for focus events from the newly added text box. When the text box loses focus, we take the current text and modify the tree item value with it:

```
public void onLostFocus(Widget sender)
{
  if (sender.isAttached())
  {
    if (!currentSelection.getText().equals(textbox.getText()))
    {
      currentSelection.setText(textbox.getText());
```

```
        }
    workPanel.remove(textbox);
    }
}
```

The isAttached() function enables us to check if the sender widget is actually attached to the root panel, or if it has already been destroyed. We avoid setting anything on the widget if it is no longer attached to the panel. That's all! GWT makes it that simple to add support for inline editing of tree nodes. The current GWT release does not yet support adding widgets other than strings to the tree as a tree item. Once that support is available, it would be simple to refactor this example to use text boxes as tree nodes, and make them editable or non-editable based on the click event.

Log Spy

In this example, we will look how a server can be polled, based on a time interval set by the client. This will involve using the GWT Timer object, and is very useful for situations where you need to perform an action on the server, based on a repeating time interval, and then asynchronously update a section of the web page with the results of the action. We will create a simple application that can monitor and display the contents of a log file in real time.

Time for Action—Updating a Log File

Almost every application has log files that contain debugging information. This information is usually read by logging in to a server, navigating to a folder containing the log file, and then opening the file in a text editor to actually view the contents. This is a tedious way of checking log files. The better and more user-friendly way is to use GWT to create an application that can display the contents of the log file in a web page. The contents are updated in real time, as messages are added to the log file. The following steps will give us the desired result:

1. Create a new Java file named LogSpyService.java in the com.packtpub. gwtbook.samples.client package. Define a LogSpyService interface with two methods—one method for retrieving all log entries and one method for retrieving only the new entries:

    ```
    public interface LogSpyService extends RemoteService
    {
      public ArrayList getAllLogEntries();
      public ArrayList getNextLogEntries();
    }
    ```

2. Create the asynchronous version of this service definition interface in a new Java file named `LogSpyServiceAsync.java` in the `com.packtpub.gwtbook.samples.client` package:

```java
public interface LogSpyServiceAsync
{
  public void getAllLogEntries(AsyncCallback callback);
  public void getNextLogEntries(AsyncCallback callback);
}
```

3. Create the implementation of the log spy service in a new Java file named `LogSpyServiceImpl.java` in the `com.packtpub.gwtbook.samples.server` package. First create a private method for reading a log file, a variable for holding the file pointer, and a variable with the name of the log file that you want to read:

```java
private long filePointer = 0;
private File logfile = new File("test2.log");
private ArrayList readLogFile()
{
  ArrayList entries = new ArrayList();
  RandomAccessFile file = new RandomAccessFile(logfile, "r");
  long fileLength = logfile.length();
  if (fileLength > filePointer)
  {
    file.seek(filePointer);
    String line = file.readLine();
    while (line != null)
    {
      line = file.readLine();
      if (line != null && line.length() > 0)
      {
        entries.add(line);
      }
    }
    filePointer = file.getFilePointer();
  }
  file.close();
  return entries;
}
```

4. Add the two methods that implement the service interface:

```java
public ArrayList getAllLogEntries()
{
  return readLogFile();
}
```

```
public ArrayList getNextLogEntries()
{
  try
  {
    Thread.sleep(1000);
  }
  catch (InterruptedException e)
  {
    e.printStackTrace();
  }
  return readLogFile();
·}
```

5. Now create the user interface for interacting with the log spy service. Create a new Java file named `LogSpyPanel.java` in the `com.packtpub.gwtbook.samples.client.panels` package. Create variables for the work panel, a text box for setting the monitoring interval, a label, and **Start** and **Stop** buttons. We will also need a Boolean flag to indicate the current status of monitoring.

```
Public VerticalPanel workPanel = new VerticalPanel();
public ListBox logSpyList = new ListBox();
public TextBox monitoringInterval = new TextBox();
public Label monitoringLabel = new Label(
                              "Monitoring Interval :");
public Button startMonitoring = new Button("Start");
public Button stopMonitoring = new Button("Stop");
private boolean isMonitoring = false;
```

6. Create panels that will contain the **Start** and **Stop** buttons, the text box and the label for the monitoring interval, and a timer:

```
private HorizontalPanel intervalPanel = new HorizontalPanel();
private HorizontalPanel startStopPanel = new HorizontalPanel();
private Timer timer;
```

7. Create a listbox for displaying the log messages, and the service interface that we will be invoking to get the log entries:

```
public ListBox logSpyList = new ListBox();
ServiceDefTarget endpoint = (ServiceDefTarget) logSpyService;
endpoint.setServiceEntryPoint GWT.getModuleBaseURL()
                              + "logspy");
```

8. In the constructor, set the initial value of the monitoring interval text box to 1000, and disable the **Stop** button:

```
monitoringInterval.setText("1000");
stopMonitoring.setEnabled(false);
```

9. Set the styles for the panels, the text box, and the label:

```
intervalPanel.setStyleName("logSpyPanel");
startStopPanel.setStyleName("logSpyStartStopPanel");
monitoringLabel.setStyleName("logSpyLabel");
monitoringInterval.setStyleName("logSpyTextbox");
```

10. Add an event handler to listen for clicks on the **Start** button, and invoke the log spy service from the handler:

```
startMonitoring.addClickListener(new ClickListener()
{
  public void onClick(Widget sender)
  {
    if (!isMonitoring)
    {
      timer = new Timer()
      {
        public void run()
        {
          AsyncCallback callback = new AsyncCallback()
          {
            public void onSuccess(Object result)
            {
              ArrayList resultItems = (ArrayList) result;
              for (Iterator iter = resultItems.iterator();
              iter.hasNext();)
              {
                logSpyList.insertItem(((String)
                                              iter.next()), 0);
                logSpyList.setSelectedIndex(0);
              }
            }
            public void onFailure(Throwable caught)
            {
              Window.alert("Error while invoking the logspy
                        service " + caught.getMessage());
            }
          };
          logSpyService.getNextLogEntries(callback);
        }
      };
      timer.scheduleRepeating(Integer.parseInt
                              (monitoringInterval.getText()));
      isMonitoring = true;
      startMonitoring.setEnabled(false);
```

```
            stopMonitoring.setEnabled(true);
        }
    }
});
```

11. Add an event handler to listen for clicks on the **Stop** button and stop monitoring:

```
stopMonitoring.addClickListener(new ClickListener()
{
  public void onClick(Widget sender)
  {
    if (isMonitoring)
    {
      timer.cancel();
      isMonitoring = false;
      startMonitoring.setEnabled(true);
      stopMonitoring.setEnabled(false);
    }
  }
});
```

12. Limit the number of visible items in the list to eight items:

```
logSpyList.setVisibleItemCount(8);
```

13. Finally, in the constructor, create a little info panel that displays descriptive text about this application, so that we can display this text when this sample is selected in the list of available samples, in our Samples application. Add the monitoring interval panel and the start-stop buttons panel to the work panel. Add the info panel and the work panel to the dock panel, and initialize the widget:

```
HorizontalPanel infoPanel = new HorizontalPanel();
infoPanel.add(new HTML
  ("<div class='infoProse'>View a log file live as entries are
      written to it. This is similar in concept to the unix
      utility tail. The new entries are retrieved and added in
      real time to the top of the list. You can start and stop
      the monitoring, and set the interval in milliseconds for
      how often you want to check the file for new entries.
      </div>"));
intervalPanel.add(monitoringLabel);
intervalPanel.add(monitoringInterval);
startStopPanel.add(startMonitoring);
startStopPanel.add(stopMonitoring);
workPanel.add(intervalPanel);
```

```
workPanel.add(startStopPanel);
workPanel.add(logSpyList);
DockPanel workPane = new DockPanel();
workPane.add(infoPanel, DockPanel.NORTH);
workPane.add(workPanel, DockPanel.CENTER);
workPane.setCellHeight(workPanel, "100%");
workPane.setCellWidth(workPanel, "100%");
initWidget(workPane);
```

14. Add the service to the module file for the `Samples` application—`Samples.gwt.xml` in the `com.packtpub.gwtbook.samples` package:

```
<servlet path="/Samples/logspy"
class="com.packtpub.gwtbook.samples.server.LogSpyServiceImpl"/>
```

Here is a screenshot of the application that displays the entries in the log file—`test.log`:

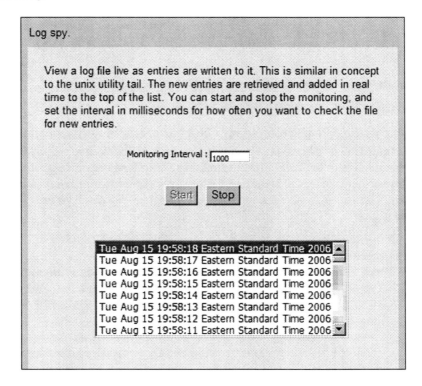

As entries are added to this file, they will be added in real time to the list, with the first item in the list being the latest log entry. You can monitor any file that you want. Just change the value of the `logFile` variable in the `LogSpyServiceImpl` class to contain the requisite file name.

What Just Happened?

Log files are usually just text files that have messages appended to them, as applications write to the log file. This sample is using a simple log file and can be modified to use any file that you want to monitor. We read the file using a RandomAccessFile class so that we can access only the sections of the file that we want, without needing to read the whole file into memory every time. A private variable that contains the last file pointer is stored in the class. This pointer is a cursor into the file. We have a method readLogFile() that accesses the file and reads only the data from the file pointer to the end of the file. Every time the file is read, the pointer is updated to store the last read position.

```
RandomAccessFile file = new RandomAccessFile(logfile, "r");
long fileLength = logfile.length();
if (fileLength > filePointer)
{
  file.seek(filePointer);
  String line = file.readLine();
  while (line != null)
  {
    line = file.readLine();
    if (line != null && line.length() > 0)
    {
      entries.add(line);
    }
  }
  filePointer = file.getFilePointer();
}
file.close();
```

If the file has not been modified since we last read it, we return an empty list without trying to read the file. Whenever the client makes a request to get the new log entries, we read the file and return the new entries.

The user interface consists of a list box, a text box that can be used to specify how often you want to monitor the log file, and buttons for starting and stopping the monitoring of the file. When the **Start** button is clicked, we start a timer that is scheduled to go off after the provided time interval. Every time the timer goes off, we make a request to get the log entries, and then in the onSuccess() callback method we add the returned entries to the listbox. We insert the log entry to the list and then set the last added entry as the selected item, so it visually indicates the latest item in the list:

```
logSpyList.insertItem(((String) iter.next()), 0);
logSpyList.setSelectedIndex(0);
```

If we click the **Stop** button, the timer is canceled, and the monitoring is halted. We do something very different here, compared to all the other samples. We call the service on a repeating time interval based on the time interval set by the user in the text box. So we make an asynchronous request every time the timer goes off. This technique can be used to do some very useful things for updating portions or sections of a page on a scheduled time interval by making synchronous calls to the server to get fresh information.

Sticky Notes

The **Document Object Model (DOM)** describes the structure of an HTML document in the form of a tree structure that can be accessed using a language such as JavaScript. All the modern web browsers facilitate the access to a loaded web page through DOM scripting. GWT provides a rich set of methods that enable you to manipulate the DOM of a web page. We can even intercept and preview DOM events. We are going to learn how to use the GWT DOM methods and dialog boxes, leverage them to provide the ability to create sticky notes similar to the ubiquitous post-it notes, and drag them around to place them anywhere in the browser window.

Time for Action—Playing with Sticky Notes

We will create sticky notes that can be moved around in your browser window and placed anywhere. The steps are as follows:

1. Create a new Java file named `StickyNotesPanel.java` in the `com.packtpub.gwtbook.samples.client.panels` package. Create a work panel, a button for creating the note, a text box for the name of the note, and variables to hold the x and y coordinates of the note. Also create an integer variable to hold the amount by which the coordinates of a new note are to be incremented:

    ```
    private HorizontalPanel workPanel = new HorizontalPanel();
    private Button createNote = new Button("Create Note");
    private TextBox noteTitle = new TextBox();
    private int noteLeft = 300;
    private int noteTop = 170;
    private int increment = 10;
    ```

2. Create a new class named `StickyNote` that extends `DialogBox`. In the constructor for this class, set the title for the note if provided, and add a text area that will be used to type in the actual note:

    ```
    public StickyNote(String title)
    {
    ```

```
      super();
      if (title.length() == 0)
      {
        setText("New Note");
      }
      else
      {
        setText(title);
      }
      TextArea text = new TextArea();
      text.setText("Type your note here");
      text.setHeight("80px");
      setWidget(text);
      setHeight("100px");
      setWidth("100px");
      setStyleName(text.getElement(), "notesText", true);
      setStyleName("notesPanel");
    }
```

3. Create a method in the `StickyNote` class that intercepts the DOM events:

```
    public boolean onEventPreview(Event event)
    {
     int type = DOM.eventGetType(event);
     switch (type)
     {
      case Event.ONKEYDOWN:
      {
        return onKeyDownPreview((char) DOM.eventGetKeyCode(event),
        KeyboardListenerCollection.getKeyboardModifiers(event));
      }
      case Event.ONKEYUP:
      {
        return onKeyUpPreview((char) DOM.eventGetKeyCode(event),
        KeyboardListenerCollection.getKeyboardModifiers(event));
      }
      case Event.ONKEYPRESS:
      {
        return onKeyPressPreview((char) DOM.eventGetKeyCode(event),
        KeyboardListenerCollection.getKeyboardModifiers(event));
      }
     }
     return true;
    }
```

4. In the constructor for the `StickyNotesPanel` class, create a little info panel that displays descriptive text about this application, so that we can display the text when this sample is selected in the list of available samples in our `Samples` application. Add this class as a listener to click events on the **Create Note** button. Add the button for creating the note along with the title text box to the work panel. Add the info panel and the work panel to the dock panel, and initialize the widget:

```
HorizontalPanel infoPanel = new HorizontalPanel();
infoPanel.add(new HTML
 ("<div class='infoProse'>Create sticky notes and drag them
     around to position any where in your browser window. Go
     ahead and try it !
   </div>"));
createNote.addClickListener(this);
createNote.setStyleName("notesButton");
workPanel.add(createNote);
noteTitle.setStyleName("notesTitle");
workPanel.add(noteTitle);
DockPanel workPane = new DockPanel();
workPane.add(infoPanel, DockPanel.NORTH);
workPane.add(workPanel, DockPanel.CENTER);
workPane.setCellHeight(workPanel, "100%");
workPane.setCellWidth(workPanel, "100%");
initWidget(workPane);
```

5. Make the `StickyNotesPanel` class implement the `ClickListener` interface, and add code to the `onClick()` method to create a new note when the **Create Note** button is clicked:

```
public void onClick(Widget sender)
{
  StickyNote note = new StickyNote(noteTitle.getText());
  note.setPopupPosition(noteLeft + increment, noteTop +
                                                increment);
  increment = increment + 40;
  note.show();
}
```

Here is a screenshot of the application:

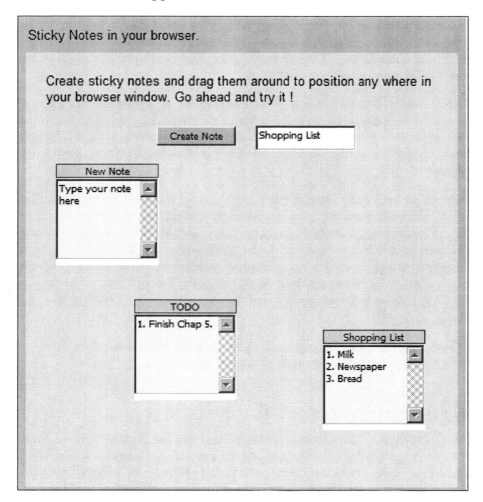

When you create several notes, you can drag the notes around and place them anywhere on the browser window.

What Just Happened?

This sample demonstrates the ease with which you can generate some really cool interfaces and applications using GWT. The sticky notes application creates notes on your screen that you can drag around inside the web browser and place anywhere you want. The user interface contains a text box for typing in the name of the note, and a button for creating a new note with the provided name. If no name is provided, it is created with a default name **New Note**.

The note itself is a subclass of `DialogBox`. It has a title and a text area for typing in the note. A `DialogBox` class inherits from a `PopupPanel` class, and implements the `EventPreview` interface. We implement the `onEventPreview()` method, as given in step 3, from this interface, so that we can preview all the browser events first, before they are sent to their targets. That essentially means that our sticky notes panel sits at the top of the browser event preview stack.

We preview the keyboard events and then pass them on, down to the target. This enables us to take a dialog box that is modal, and introduce non-modal behavior to it. If we do not do this, once we create the first note, the note will be modal, and will not allow us to create another note by clicking on the **Create** button, unless we close the note first.

Now the note passes on the events after previewing them to the underlying panel, and we can create as many notes as we want. An event handler is registered to listen for clicks on the **Create Note** button. When the button is clicked, a new note is created and we set its position relative to the browser window, and then show it. We maintain a private variable that contains the left position of the last created note, so that we can stagger the position of the notes as we create them, as we have done in step 5. This arranges the notes nicely on the screen so that the notes do not cover each other.

As our notes inherit from `DialogBox`, they are draggable; we can drag them around the screen, and position them anywhere we want!

Jigsaw Puzzle

The previous sample demonstrated some of the dragging capabilities and DOM event previewing in GWT. In this example, we are going to use the same DOM methods but a different way to intercept or preview the DOM events. We will also demonstrate some of the absolute positioning capabilities in GWT by using `AbsolutePanel`. We will be creating a simple Mona Lisa puzzle that can be solved by dragging and rearranging the pieces of the puzzle.

Time for Action—Let's Create a Puzzle!

We will create a simple jigsaw puzzle, whose pieces were created by dividing a Mona Lisa image into nine pieces. The steps are as follows:

1. Create a new Java file named `JigsawPuzzlePanel.java` in the `com.packtpub.gwtbook.samples.client.panels` package that implements the `MouseListener` interface. Create an `AbsolutePanel` class that will be the main panel to which all the widgets will be added. Also add two variables to store the x and y positions of the mouse cursor:

```
private AbsolutePanel workPanel = new AbsolutePanel();
private boolean inDrag;
private int xOffset;
private int yOffset;
```

2. In the constructor for `JigsawPuzzlePanel`, add the Mona Lisa images to the panel, and add the panel as a listener for mouse events from the images:

```
Image monalisa = new Image("images/monalisa_face1_8.jpg");
monalisa.addMouseListener(this);
workPanel.add(monalisa, 60, 20);
monalisa = new Image("images/monalisa_face1_7.jpg");
monalisa.addMouseListener(this);
workPanel.add(monalisa, 60, 125);
monalisa = new Image("images/monalisa_face1_2.jpg");
monalisa.addMouseListener(this);
workPanel.add(monalisa, 60, 230);
monalisa = new Image("images/monalisa_face1_3.jpg");
monalisa.addMouseListener(this);
workPanel.add(monalisa, 170, 20);
monalisa = new Image("images/monalisa_face1_4.jpg");
monalisa.addMouseListener(this);
workPanel.add(monalisa, 170, 125);
monalisa = new Image("images/monalisa_face1_1.jpg");
monalisa.addMouseListener(this);
workPanel.add(monalisa, 170, 230);
monalisa = new Image("images/monalisa_face1_6.jpg");
monalisa.addMouseListener(this);
workPanel.add(monalisa, 280, 20);
monalisa = new Image("images/monalisa_face1_9.jpg");
monalisa.addMouseListener(this);
workPanel.add(monalisa, 280, 125);
monalisa = new Image("images/monalisa_face1_5.jpg");
monalisa.addMouseListener(this);
workPanel.add(monalisa, 280, 230);
```

3. Register to intercept the DOM mouse events in the constructor:

```
DOM.addEventPreview(new EventPreview()
{
  public boolean onEventPreview(Event event)
  {
    switch (DOM.eventGetType(event))
    {
      case Event.ONMOUSEDOWN:
      case Event.ONMOUSEMOVE:
```

```
            case Event.ONMOUSEUP:
               DOM.eventPreventDefault(event);
            }
            return true;
         }
      });
```

4. Implement the method to listen for mouse down events in the constructor:

```
public void onMouseDown(Widget source, int x, int y)
{
   DOM.setCapture(source.getElement());
   xOffset = x;
   yOffset = y;
   inDrag = true;
}
```

5. Implement the method to listen for mouse move events in the constructor:

```
public void onMouseMove(Widget source, int x, int y)
{
   if (inDrag)
   {
      int xAbs = x + source.getAbsoluteLeft() - 135;
      int yAbs = y + source.getAbsoluteTop() - 120;
      ((AbsolutePanel)source.getParent()).
      setWidgetPosition(source,  xAbs- xOffset, yAbs - yOffset);
   }
}
```

6. Implement the method to listen for mouse up events in the constructor:

```
public void onMouseUp(Widget source, int x, int y)
{
   DOM.releaseCapture(source.getElement());
   inDrag = false;
}
```

7. Finally in the constructor, create a little info panel that displays descriptive text about this application, so that we can display the text when this sample is selected in the list of available samples in our Samples application. Add the info panel and the work panel to the dock panel, and initialize the widget:

```
HorizontalPanel infoPanel = new HorizontalPanel();
infoPanel.add(new HTML
  ("<div class='infoProse'>This example demonstrates the use
     of dragging to move things around and place them anywhere
```

```
    in the window. It is easy to forget that you are actually
    doing this in a web browser !
    </div>"));
DockPanel workPane = new DockPanel();
workPane.add(infoPanel, DockPanel.NORTH);
workPane.add(workPanel, DockPanel.CENTER);
workPane.setCellHeight(workPanel, "100%");
workPane.setCellWidth(workPanel, "100%");
initWidget(workPane);
```

Here is the puzzle when you first visit the page:

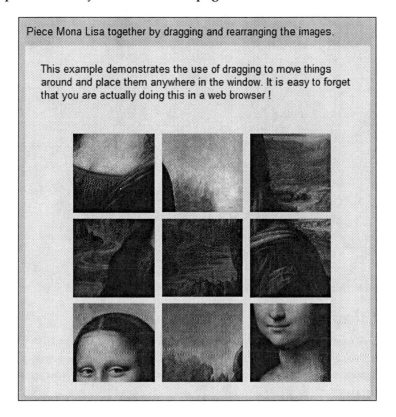

Here is the solved puzzle:

What Just Happened?

This sample demonstrates the absolute positioning capabilities in GWT. An image file of the Mona Lisa was split into nine equal-sized images. We jumble the images and present them on the screen in a 3x3 square, when the application is rendered. The user can then rearrange the image pieces by dragging them around and repositioning them on the screen to recreate the Mona Lisa.

We use an AbsolutePanel class as our work panel in this sample. It has the ability to position all of its child widgets absolutely, and even allows the widgets to overlap. We add the nine images to the panel by positioning them absolutely, so they form a nice 3x3 grid.

Here is one column of the grid:

```
Image monalisa = new Image("images/monalisa_face1_8.jpg");
monalisa.addMouseListener(this);
workPanel.add(monalisa, 60, 20);
monalisa = new Image("images/monalisa_face1_7.jpg");
monalisa.addMouseListener(this);
workPanel.add(monalisa, 60, 125);
monalisa = new Image("images/monalisa_face1_2.jpg");
monalisa.addMouseListener(this);
workPanel.add(monalisa, 60, 230);
```

In the previous example, we were able to implement the `onEventpreview()` method to preview the browser events first before they are sent to their target. We were able to do this as the note was a subclass of `PopupPanel`, which provides this ability. But in the current sample we are not using a pop-up panel. So we use another method to add ourselves to the top of the event preview stack. This time we are using the `addEvetnpreview()` method in the DOM object, as illustrated in step 3.

In step 4, we implement the `MouseListener` interface and register ourselves as the event handler for mouse events in the panel. When the user clicks on an image prior to dragging it, we get the element that was clicked and set it as the mouse-capture. This ensures that element will receive all of the mouse events, until it is released from the mouse-capture. We store the x and y coordinates of the element in a private variable. We also set a flag that tells us that we are currently in the mode of dragging an element.

Once the user starts dragging an image, we check to see if we are in drag mode, and we set the position of the widget, which will move the widget to the new position. You can only set the absolute widget position by calling the absolute panel that contains the widget; so we have to get the parent object of the image and then cast it to the right class. We have covered all this in step 5.

When the user has finished dragging an image to a position and releasing the mouse, we release the element from the mouse-capture and set the drag flag to false, as in step 6.

The absolute positioning support in GWT still needs some work, and can act quite different in Firefox and Internet Explorer, and their multiple versions.

Summary

In this chapter, we learned how to create tables that can page through a set of data in a user-friendly manner, and extended a tree widget to add simple support for editing the tree nodes in place. We utilized the `timer` object to create a log spy application that monitors a given log file for new entries, and displays them in a list that is updated in real time.

We learned how to use some of the DOM methods and the DOM event preview capability in GWT, and leveraged it to implement a draggable sticky notes application. We also learned how to make dialog boxes non-modal, so that we can adapt them for our use. Finally, utilizing the absolute positioning functionality and an alternate method of previewing DOM events, we created a puzzle application.

In the next chapter, we will learn how to integrate third-party JavaScript libraries with GWT using the JavaScript Native Interface.

6

Browser Effects with JSNI and JavaScript Libraries

In this chapter, we will learn how to create user interfaces that can utilize cool browser effects provided by some well-known third-party JavaScript libraries. We will take advantage of the JavaScript Native Interface (JSNI) provided by GWT to wrap these existing JavaScript libraries and use them in our GWT applications.

The tasks that we will address are:

- Moo.Fx
- Rico Rounded Corners
- Rico Color Selector
- Script.aculo.us effects

What is JSNI?

JSNI provides a way to mix JavaScript code with Java code. It is similar in concept to the Java Native Interface (JNI) provided by Sun's Java environment. JNI enables your Java code to call C and C++ methods. JSNI enables your Java code to call into JavaScript methods. It is very powerful technique that lets us access low-level JavaScript code directly from Java code, and opens the door to a wide variety of uses and possibilities listed below:

- Call JavaScript code from Java
- Call Java code from JavaScript
- Throw exceptions that cross the Java/JavaScript boundaries
- Access Java fields from JavaScript

However, this powerful technique should be used carefully, as JSNI code may not be portable across browsers. The current implementation of the GWT compiler will also not be able to perform any optimizations on JSNI code. JSNI methods must always be declared native, and the JavaScript code that is placed in the JSNI method must be placed in a comment block that is specially formatted. So each JSNI method will consist of two parts—a native method declaration, and the JavaScript code for the method embedded inside a specially formatted code block. Here is an example of a JSNI method that calls the `alert()` JavaScript method:

```
native void helloGWTBook()
/*-{
  $wnd.alert("Hello, GWT book!");
}-*/;
```

In the above example, the JavaScript code is embedded in a '/*-{' and '}-*/' block. Another thing to be aware of is the use of the $wnd and $doc variables. GWT code always runs inside a nested frame inside the browser, so you cannot access the window or document objects in the normal way inside your JSNI code. You must use the $wnd and $doc variables, which are automatically initialized by GWT to refer to the window and document objects for the host page. The GWT compiler can check our JSNI code. So if you run it in web mode and compile your application, the compiler will flag any errors in your JSNI code. This is a nice way to debug JSNI code, as these errors will not be displayed until run time when you are running in hosted mode. In this chapter, we are going to use JSNI to wrap some third-party JavaScript libraries, and use the cool browser effects provided by them, inside our GWT user interfaces.

 In the recent versions of GWT, JSNI functions sometimes do not work in hosted mode, but work fine when deployed.

Moo.Fx

Moo.fx is a super lightweight and fast JavaScript library that provides several cool effects for web applications (http://moofx.mad4milk.net). It is compact and works in all the major web browsers. We are going to use JSNI to wrap some of the effects provided by the Moo.fx library and use these effects in our GWT application.

Time for Action—Using JSNI

We are going to use the JSNI provided by the GWT framework to wrap the `Moo.fx` library and intermingle Java and JavaScript to use its functionality in our GWT user interface.

1. Add the prototype and `Moo.fx` JavaScript files that will be needed by our application to the module's HTML file—`Samples.html`.

    ```
    <script type="text/JavaScript"src="JavaScript/prototype.js">
    </script>
    <script type="text/JavaScript"src="JavaScript/moo.fx.js">
    </script>
    ```

2. Create a new Java class named `MooFx.java` in the `com.packtpub.gwtbook.samples.client.util` package that wraps the `Moo.fx` JavaScript library effects.

3. Add a new JSNI method in `MooFx.java` for creating an `opacity.fx` object.

    ```
    public native static Element opacity(Element element)
    /*-{
      $wnd._nativeExtensions = false;
      return new $wnd.fx.Opacity(element);
    }-*/;
    ```

4. Add a JSNI method for toggling the opacity effect.

    ```
    public native static void toggleOpacity(Element element)
    /*-{
      $wnd._nativeExtensions = false;
      element.toggle();
    }-*/;
    ```

5. Add a private JSNI method that takes a parameter string of options and converts it into a JavaScript object.

    ```
    private static native JavaScriptObject buildOptions
                                                    (String opts)
    /*-{
      eval("var optionObject = new Object()");
      var options = opts.split(',');
      for (var i =0; i < options.length; i++)
        {
          var opt = options[i].split(':');
          eval("optionObject." + opt[0] + "=" +  opt[1]);
        }
      return optionObject;
    }-*/;
    ```

6. Add a static Java method for creating a height effect, which uses the above `buildOptions()` to build a JavaScript object for passing on the options to a JSNI method.

```
public static Element height(Element element, String opts)
{
  return height(element, buildOptions(opts));
}
```

7. Add a new JSNI method that will create the height effect object.

```
private native static Element height
                        (Element element, JavaScriptObject opts)
/*-{
  $wnd._nativeExtensions = false;
  return new $wnd.fx.Height(element, opts);
}-*/;
```

8. Add a new JSNI method for toggling the height effect.

```
public native static void toggleHeight(Element element)
/*-{
  $wnd._nativeExtensions = false;
  element.toggle();
  }-*/;
```

9. Add a static Java method for creating a width effect, which uses the above `buildOptions()` to build a JavaScript object for passing on the options to a JSNI method.

```
public static Element width(Element element, String opts)
{
  return width(element, buildOptions(opts));
}
```

10. Add a new JSNI method that will create the width effect object.

```
private native static Element width
                        (Element element, JavaScriptObject opts)
/*-{
  $wnd._nativeExtensions = false;
  return new $wnd.fx.Width(element, opts);
}-*/;
```

11. Add a new JSNI method for toggling the width effect.

```
public native static void toggleWidth(Element element)
/*-{
  $wnd._nativeExtensions = false;
  element.toggle();
}-*/;
```

12. Create the user interface for this application in a new Java file named MooFxEffectsPanel.java in the com.packtpub.gwtbook.samples. client.panels package. Add an HTML fragment that contains an outer div element with an inner div element that contains a paragraph element with text. Add three different variables containing this fragment. Also add an element for each effect.

```java
private HTML opacityBox = new HTML
                ("<div class='moofxBox'><div id=\"opacitybox\">
    <p class=\"text\">
      Lorem ipsum dolor sit amet, consectetur adipisicing elit,
      sed do eiusmod tempor incididunt ut labore et dolore
      magna aliqua. Ut enim ad minim veniam, quis nostrud
      exercitation ullamco laboris nisi ut aliquip ex ea
      commodo consequat.
    </p></div></div>");
private HTML heightBox = new HTML
                ("<div class='moofxBox'><div id=\"heightbox\">
    <p class=\"text\">
      Lorem ipsum dolor sit amet, consectetur adipisicing elit,
      sed do eiusmod tempor incididunt ut labore et dolore
      magna aliqua. Ut enim ad minim veniam, quis nostrud
      exercitation ullamco laboris nisi ut aliquip ex ea
      commodo consequat.
    </p></div></div>");
private HTML widthBox = new HTML
                ("<div class='moofxBox'><div id=\"widthbox\">
    <p class=\"text\">
      Lorem ipsum dolor sit amet, consectetur adipisicing elit,
      sed do eiusmod tempor incididunt ut labore et dolore
      magna aliqua. Ut enim ad minim veniam, quis nostrud
      exercitation ullamco laboris nisi ut aliquip ex ea
      commodo consequat.
    </p></div></div>");
private Element widthBoxElement;
private Element heightBoxElement;
private Element opacityBoxElement;
```

13. Create three buttons, one for toggling each Moo.fx effect.

```java
Button opacityButton = new Button("Toggle Opacity");
Button heightButton = new Button("Toggle Height");
Button widthButton = new Button("Toggle Width");
```

14. Register an event handler to listen for clicks on each of the buttons, and call the appropriate method for toggling the effect.

```
opacityButton.addClickListener(new ClickListener()
                        {
                          public void onClick(Widget sender)
                          {
                            MooFx.toggleOpacity
                                      (opacityBoxElement);
                          }
                        });
heightButton.addClickListener(new ClickListener()
                        {
                          public void onClick(Widget sender)
                          {
                            MooFx.toggleHeight
                                      (heightBoxElement);
                          }
                        });
widthButton.addClickListener(new ClickListener()
                        {
                          public void onClick(Widget sender)
                          {
                            MooFx.toggleWidth
                                      (widthBoxElement);
                          }
                        });
```

15. Create a `DeferredCommand` that creates each of the effect objects when it executes.

```
DeferredCommand.add(new Command()
                    {
                      public void execute()
                      {
                        opacityBoxElement = MooFx.opacity
                            (DOM.getElementById("opacitybox"));
                      }
                    });
DeferredCommand.add(new Command()
                    {
                      public void execute()
                      {
                        heightBoxElement =
                                MooFx.height(DOM.getElementById
                                ("heightbox"), "duration:2500");
```

```
                          }
                        });
     DeferredCommand.add(new Command()
                        {
                          public void execute()
                          {
                            widthBoxElement =
                                      MooFx.width(DOM.getElementById
                                      ("widthbox"), "duration:2000");
                          }
                        });
```

16. In the constructor, add the buttons and divs for each effect to the work panel.

```
     opacityButton.setStyleName("moofxButton");
     workPanel.add(opacityButton);
     workPanel.add(opacityBox);
     heightButton.setStyleName("moofxButton");
     workPanel.add(heightButton);
     workPanel.add(heightBox);
     widthButton.setStyleName("moofxButton");
     workPanel.add(widthButton);
     workPanel.add(widthBox);
```

17. Finally, create a little info panel that displays descriptive text about this application, so that we can display this text when this sample is selected in the list of available samples in our Samples application. Add the info panel and the work panel to a dock panel, and initialize the widget.

```
     HorizontalPanel infoPanel = new HorizontalPanel();
        infoPanel.add(new HTML("<div class='infoProse'>
                                Use cool Moo.fx effects in your
                                    GWT application.</div>"));
     DockPanel workPane - new DockPanel();
     workPane.add(infoPanel, DockPanel.NORTH);
     workPane.add(workPanel, DockPanel.CENTER);
     workPane.setCellHeight(workPanel, "100%");
     workPane.setCellWidth(workPanel, "100%");
     initWidget(workPane);
```

Here is a screenshot of the application. Click on each button to see the effect in action.

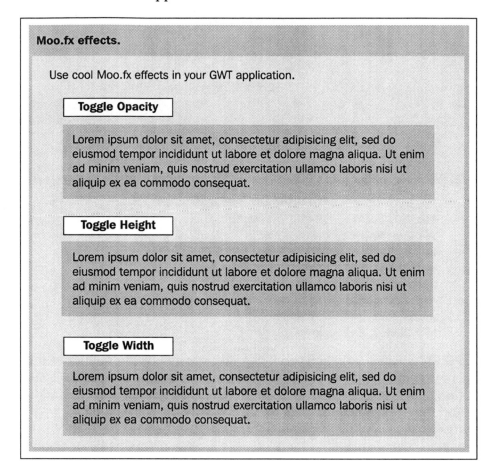

What Just Happened?

The main effects provided by the Moo.fx library are:

- Opacity: Modify the opacity or transparency of an element.
- Height: Modify the height of an element.
- Width: Modify the width of an element.

In this sample, we created a Java class named MooFx, which wrapped the Moo.fx JavaScript library using JSNI. We created a native method named opacity() for instantiating an opacity object. In this method, we call the JavaScript constructor for the opacity object and return the resulting object, which is of type Element. We store this in a variable.

```
return new $wnd.fx.Opacity(element);
```

We then create a native method named `toggleOpacity()` for toggling the opacity of an element from one state to another. This method uses the variable that we stored earlier and calls the toggle method on it to change its current state.

```
element.toggle();
```

We create `height()` and `width()` Java methods that are passed a string parameter containing the options that need to be provided to the `Moo.fx` height and width constructors. These two methods use a native method named `buildOptions()` to create the JavaScript object containing the options, which will then be passed on to the native method for creating the height and width. The `buildOptions()` method parses the provided string, and creates a JavaScript object and sets its properties and the property values. We again utilize the `eval()` function to set the properties and return the object.

```
private static native JavaScriptObject buildOptions(String opts)
/*-{
  eval("var optionObject = new Object()");
  var options = opts.split(',');
  for (var i =0; i < options.length; i++)
  {
    var opt = options[i].split(':');
    eval("optionObject." + opt[0] + "=" + opt[1]);
  }
  return optionObject;
}-*/;
```

The returned JavaScript options object is passed on to the native `height()` and `width()` methods to create the respective effect objects similar to the `opacity()` method. We then add native methods for toggling the height and width. That is all we have to do to wrap the library in an easy-to-use Java class!

In the user interface, we create an HTML object with an outer `div` that contains an inner `div` with a paragraph of text. The HTML widget enables us to create arbitrary HTML and add it to a panel. We used the HTML widget in this sample, but we can also create the same element using the methods in the DOM object in the GWT framework. In the next sample, we will use that functionality, so that we are familiar with the different tools provided by GWT. We also create three buttons, one each for toggling each of the effects. Event handlers are registered with each of these buttons to listen for clicks and then call the appropriate toggle method for the specified effect. In the method for creating the effect, we use the `getElementById()` on the DOM object to get the `div` element that we are interested in. We needed to do this, as we do not have access to the `div` that we added to the panel. The `div` that we were interested in was added to the panel as part of the HTML widget.

```
opacityBoxElement = MooFx.opacity(DOM.getElementById("opacitybox"));
```

We then toggle the requisite effect on the element.

```
MooFx.toggleOpacity(opacityBoxElement);
```

The effects themselves are constructed by calling the respective constructors for the effects inside DeferredCommand. The elements that we have added are not available yet by using their ID, until the event handlers have all completed. The DeferredCommand runs after they have all completed, and this ensures that our element has been added to the DOM and can be accessed by using its ID. We get the element, create an effect, and associate it with the element.

```
DeferredCommand.add(new Command()
                 {
                   public void execute()
                   {
                     opacityBoxElement = MooFx.opacity
                               (DOM.getElementById("opacitybox"));
                   }
                 });
```

We have successfully accessed the library from Java in our GWT application, and can reuse these effects everywhere. In the ColorSelector sample later in this chapter, we will use one of the Moo.fx effects in combination with effects form other libraries.

Rico Rounded Corners

Elements on a web page with rounded corners are visually much more attractive than straight corners and are aesthetically more appealing. It is also one of the hottest design trends in the look and feel of web applications. Rico (http://openrico. org/rico/home.page) is another fine JavaScript library that has great support for this and makes it extremely easy to use. It also provides a great deal of functionality, but we are only wrapping and using the rounded corners effects part of Rico. We are only using labels in this sample for applying the rounded corners, but you can also apply it to text paragraphs and several other HTML elements. In this example we will wrap the rounded corners effect from Rico and use it in our application to display several labels with different types of rounded corners.

Time for Action—Supporting the Labels

We are going to wrap the Rico library and provide support for labels with rounded corners in our GWT user interface.

1. Add the prototype and Rico JavaScript files that will be needed by our application to the module's HTML file—Samples.html.

```
<script type="text/JavaScript"src="JavaScript/prototype.js">
</script>
<script type="text/JavaScript"src="JavaScript/rico.fx.js">
</script>
```

2. Create a new Java class named `Rico.java` in the `com.packtpub.gwtbook.samples.client.util` package that will wrap the `rico` JavaScript library effects.

3. Add a new JSNI method in `Rico.java` for rounding the corner of a widget.

```
private native static void corner
                        (Element element, JavaScriptObject opts)
/*-{
  $wnd._nativeExtensions = false;
  $wnd.Rico.Corner.round(element, opts);
}-*/;
```

4. Add a private JSNI method that takes a parameter of string options and converts it into a JavaScript object.

```
private static native JavaScriptObject buildOptions(String opts)
/*-{
  eval("var optionObject = new Object()");
  var options = opts.split(',');
  for (var i =0; i < options.length; i++)
  {
    var opt = options[i].split(':');
    eval("optionObject." + opt[0] + "=" + opt[1]);
  }
  return optionObject;
}-*/;
```

5. Add a static Java method for creating a rounded corner, which uses the above `buildOptions()` to build a JavaScript object for passing on the options to a JSNI method.

```
public static void corner(Widget widget, String opts)
{
  corner(widget.getElement(), buildOptions(opts));
}
```

6. Add a static Java method for creating a rounded corner without passing any options, and using the defaults.

```
public static void corner(Widget widget)
{
  corner(widget.getElement(), null);
}
```

7. Create the user interface for this application in a new Java file named
   `RoundedCornersPanel.java` in the `com.packtpub.gwtbook.samples.`
   `client.panels` package. Create a grid with three rows and two columns.
   We will add labels to this grid.

   ```
   private Grid grid = new Grid(3, 2);
   ```

8. Add six labels that will have six different rounded corners applied to them.

   ```
   private Label lbl1 = new Label("Label with rounded corners.");
   private Label lbl2 = new Label
                        ("Label with only the top corners rounded.");
   private Label lbl3 = new Label("Label with only the
                                   bottom corners rounded.");
   private Label lbl4 = new Label("Label with only the
                                   bottom right corner rounded.");
   private Label lbl5 = new Label("Label with compact
                                   rounded corners ");
   private Label lbl6 = new Label("Label with rounded corners
                                   and red border.");
   ```

9. Call the method to create the rounded corner for each of the labels, passing it
   different options to it.

   ```
   Rico.corner(lbl1);
   Rico.corner(lbl2, "corners:\"top\"");
   Rico.corner(lbl3, "corners:\"bottom\"");
   Rico.corner(lbl4, "corners:\"br\"");
   Rico.corner(lbl5, "compact:true");
   Rico.corner(lbl6, "border: 'red'");
   ```

10. Add the labels to the grid.

    ```
    grid.setWidget(0, 0, lbl1);
    grid.setWidget(0, 1, lbl2);
    grid.setWidget(1, 0, lbl3);
    grid.setWidget(1, 1, lbl4);
    grid.setWidget(2, 0, lbl5);
    grid.setWidget(2, 1, lbl6);
    ```

11. Finally, create a little info panel that displays descriptive text about this
    application, so that we can display this text when this sample is selected in
    the list of available samples in our `Samples` application. Add the info panel
    and the work panel to a dock panel, and initialize the widget.

    ```
    HorizontalPanel infoPanel =
                    new HorizontalPanel();infoPanel.add(new HTML
                    ("<div class='infoProse'>Labels with different
                            kinds of rounded corners.</div>"));
    workPanel.add(grid);
    ```

```
DockPanel workPane = new DockPanel();
workPane.add(infoPanel, DockPanel.NORTH);
workPane.add(workPanel, DockPanel.CENTER);
workPane.setCellHeight(workPanel, "100%");
workPane.setCellWidth(workPanel, "100%");
initWidget(workPane);
```

Here is a screenshot displaying labels with different types of rounded corners:

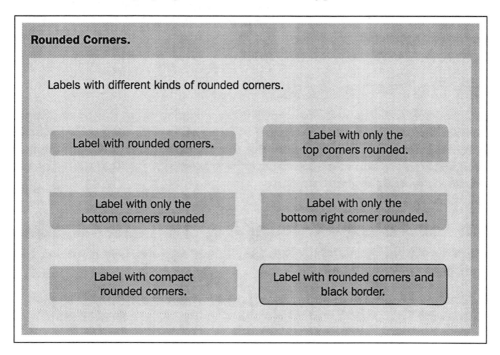

What Just Happened?

We created a Java class that uses JSNI to provide access to the rounded corners functionality in the `Rico` JavaScript library. We create a `buildOptions()` method like in the previous sample, which can accept a parameter that contains a string with options, and add those options as properties on a native JavaScript object. This options object is then passed to a JSNI method that calls the `corner()` method in the Rico library for the provided element.

```
private native static void corner
                             (Element element, JavaScriptObject opts)
/*-{
  $wnd._nativeExtensions = false;
  $wnd.Rico.Corner.round(element, opts);
}-*/;
```

In the user interface, we create a grid, and add six labels to it. Each of these labels has a different type of rounded corner applied to it. Rico supports rounded corners on all four sides or a specific side. It can also create corners in the compact form, where the corners are slightly less rounded than the default version. You can even round two or three corners and leave the fourth one square. Rico provides other methods that you can wrap and use in your application in addition to the rounded corners. The procedure is very similar to what we have done so far and is usually just a matter of implementing all the methods from the JavaScript library that you are interested in. In the next sample, we will wrap some more functionality in Rico and use it in a color selector application.

Rico Color Selector

We have successfully wrapped the rounded corners effect from Rico in the previous example. In this section, we are going to add support for accessing color information using Rico's Color object. We will wrap this functionality using JSNI and then create a color selector application that uses Rico color objects along with the Moo.fx effects that we created earlier in the chapter.

Time for Action—Wrapping the Color Methods

We will wrap the `color` methods in the `Rico` library and use them to create an application for selecting colors.

1. Add a new JSNI method in `Rico.java` for creating a `color` object with provided `red`, `green`, and `blue` values, and apply it to the element provided.

```
public native static void color
                    (Element element, int red, int green,int blue)
/*-{
  $wnd._nativeExtensions = false;
  eval('' + element.id  +' = new $wnd.Rico.Color
                          (' + red +',' + green +',' + blue + ')');
                          element.style.backgroundColor=eval
                                    (element.id + '.asHex()');
}-*/;
```

2. Add a new JSNI method in `Rico.java` for getting the hex value of a Rico color object.

```
public native static String getColorAsHex(Element element)
/*-{
  $wnd._nativeExtensions = false;
  return (eval(element.id + '.asHex()'));
}-*/;
```

3. Create the user interface for this application in a new Java file named `ColorSelectorPanel.java` in the `com.packtpub.gwtbook.samples.client.panels` package. Create a grid with three rows and three columns. Create three text fields for entering the values, along with the work panel and `div`s for the color box and the color text.

```java
private HorizontalPanel workPanel = new HorizontalPanel();
private Grid grid = new Grid(3, 3);
private TextBox redText = new TextBox();
private TextBox greenText = new TextBox();
private TextBox blueText = new TextBox();
private Element outerDiv = DOM.createDiv();
private Element colorDiv = DOM.createDiv();
private Element colorText = DOM.createElement("P");
private Element colorBox = DOM.createElement("P");
```

4. In the constructor, initialize the grid, and default the values in each of the text boxes to zero.

```java
grid.setText(0, 0, "Red");
grid.setText(1, 0, "Green");
grid.setText(2, 0, "Blue");
redText.setText("0");
grid.setWidget(0, 1, redText);
greenText.setText("0");
grid.setWidget(1, 1, greenText);
blueText.setText("0");
grid.setWidget(2, 1, blueText);
grid.setText(0, 2, "(0-255)");
grid.setText(1, 2, "(0-255)");
grid.setText(2, 2, "(0-255)");
```

5. Register an event handler to listen for keyboard events.

```java
redText.addKeyboardListener(this);
blueText.addKeyboardListener(this);
greenText.addKeyboardListener(this);
```

6. Create a paragraph element for displaying the selected color.

```java
DOM.setAttribute(colorBox, "className", "ricoColorBox");
DOM.setAttribute(colorBox, "id", "colorBox");
DOM.setInnerText(colorBox, "");
Rico.color(colorBox, 0, 0, 0);
```

7. Create the element for displaying the hex value of the selected color.

```java
DOM.setAttribute(outerDiv, "className", "heightBox");
DOM.setAttribute(colorDiv, "id", "colorDiv");
```

```
   DOM.setAttribute(colorText, "className", "text");
   DOM.appendChild(colorDiv, colorText);
   DOM.appendChild(outerDiv, colorDiv);
   DOM.appendChild(workPanel.getElement(), outerDiv);
```

8. Create a `DeferredCommand` for initializing the height effect from `Moo.fx` and for setting the initial selected color as (0, 0, 0).

```
DeferredCommand.add(new Command()
{
  public void execute()
  {
    MooFx.height(DOM.getElementById("colorDiv"),
                                            "duration:500");
    DOM.setInnerText(colorText, Rico.getColorAsHex
                                            (colorBox));
  }
});
```

9. Add an `onKeyPress()` handler to display the selected color when the user types in the new RGB values, and apply the height effect to the `div` displaying the hex value of the selected color.

```
public void onKeyPress(Widget sender, char keyCode,
                                            int modifiers)
{
  MooFx.toggleHeight(DOM.getElementById("colorDiv"));
  Timer t = new Timer()
  {
    public void run()
    {
      if ((redText.getText().length() > 0)
                        && (greenText.getText().length() > 0)
                        && (blueText.getText().length() > 0))
      {
        Rico.color(colorBox,
                        Integer.parseInt(redText.getText()),
                        Integer.parseInt(greenText.getText()),
                        Integer.parseInt(blueText.getText()));
        DOM.setInnerText(colorText, Rico.getColorAsHex
                                            (colorBox));
        MooFx.toggleHeight(DOM.getElementById("colorDiv"));
      }
    }
  };
  t.schedule(500);
}
```

10. Finally, create a little info panel that displays descriptive text about this application, so that we can display this text when this sample is selected in the list of available samples in our `Samples` application. Add the info panel and the work panel to a dock panel, and initialize the widget.

```
HorizontalPanel infoPanel = new HorizontalPanel();infoPanel.add
    (new HTML("<div class='infoProse'>
    Select a color by providing the red, green and blue values.
    The selected color will be applied to the box on the screen
    and the hex value of the color will be displayed below it
    with an element sliding up and then sliding down to display
    the value. Check it out by typing in the color
    components!</div>"));
DockPanel workPane = new DockPanel();
workPane.add(infoPanel, DockPanel.NORTH);
workPane.add(workPanel, DockPanel.CENTER);
workPane.setCellHeight(workPanel, "100%");
workPane.setCellWidth(workPanel, "100%");
initWidget(workPane);
```

Here is the application. Type in new values of RGB, and watch the selected color being displayed as soon as you stop typing, and the hex value for the current color displayed with a slide up and slide down window effect!

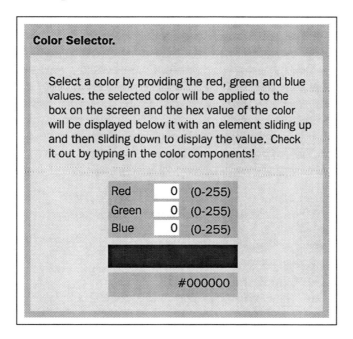

What Just Happened?

We first enhance our Rico wrapper class from the previous sample, to add access to the color functionality. Rico provides us with the ability to create a color object by using a set of red, green, and blue values. Once this color object is constructed, its hex value can be retrieved as a string. We add a JSNI method to create a color object. Inside this method, we create the `Rico.Color` object and then set the background of the provided element to the newly created color. The color object is stored in a variable with the name of the variable being the same as the ID of the element. We use the `eval()` method to dynamically create the variable and to set the background color. We set the `backgroundColor` DHTML property for the element:

```
eval('' + element.id  +' = new $wnd.Rico.Color
                      (' + red +',' + green +',' + blue + ')');
element.style.backgroundColor=eval(element.id + '.asHex()');
```

We also create a JSNI method that can return the hex value of the background color of the provided element.

```
public native static String getColorAsHex(Element element)
/*-{
  return (eval(element.id + '.asHex()'));
}-*/;
```

In the user interface, we create a grid and populate it with three text boxes for entering the color values, and some identifiers for each field. We use the DOM object for creating various elements in this sample, instead of using an HTML widget. The DOM object contains several static methods for creating various elements and for manipulating the Document Object Model of the web page. We create two `div` elements and a paragraph element and add them to the panel in the page. These will be used for creating the element that will have the height effect applied to it to slide up and down the `div` before displaying the hex value of the selected color. Since the `workPanel` is a GWT widget, we call the `getElement()` method provided on all the widgets to get access to the underlying DOM element, and then append the `div` element to it.

```
DOM.setAttribute(outerDiv, "className", "heightBox");
DOM.setAttribute(colorDiv, "id", "colorDiv");
DOM.setAttribute(colorText, "className", "text");
DOM.appendChild(colorDiv, colorText);
DOM.appendChild(outerDiv, colorDiv);
DOM.appendChild(workPanel.getElement(), outerDiv);
```

We once again use a `DeferredCommand` to set the initial hex value of the current color and to set up the height effect object from `Moo.fx`. Since we are using a paragraph element to display the string with the color hex value, we have to set its inner text using the DOM object. If we used a GWT widget instead, we would set the value by calling the `setText()` method.

```
MooFx.height(DOM.getElementById("colorDiv"), "duration:500");
DOM.setInnerText(colorText, Rico.getColorAsHex(colorBox));
```

Finally, in the `onKeyPress()` method we first toggle the height of the `colordiv`, so the element slides up. Then we schedule a timer to go off in 500 milliseconds, and when the timer fires, we create a new color object with the current values in the red, green, and blue text boxes, set the text of the `colorText` element to the hex value of this color, and then toggle the height of the `colordiv` so it slides down to display this value. The timer is necessary to slow it down a little, so you can clearly see the transition and the effect.

```
MooFx.toggleHeight(DOM.getElementById("colorDiv"));
Timer t = new Timer()
{
  public void run()
  {
    if((redText.getText().length() > 0)
                            && (greenText.getText().length() > 0)
                            && (blueText.getText().length() > 0))
    {
      Rico.color(colorBox, Integer.parseInt(redText.getText()),
      Integer.parseInt(greenText.getText()),
                          Integer.parseInt(blueText.getText()));
      DOM.setInnerText(colorText, Rico.getColorAsHex(colorBox));
      MooFx.toggleHeight(DOM.getElementById("colorDiv"));
    }
  }
};
t.schedule(500);
```

Script.aculo.us Effects

`Script.aculo.us` (http://script.aculo.us/) is an amazing JavaScript library written by Thomas Fuchs that enables all kinds of snazzy transitions and visual effects inside the web page. It is a cross-browser-compatible library that is built on top of the prototype JavaScript framework. It is also one of the most popular Web 2.0 libraries that is widely used in a variety of applications and is, most notably, also included in the Ruby On Rails web framework. `Script.aculo.us` effects are integrated and provided by the `Effect` class, which is a part of this library. We will use this class to invoke and use the various effects in our GWT application. Unlike the other sections in this chapter, we will not use JSNI here, but we will show how to use an existing wrapper library inside our application to provide some nice browser effects.

Time for Action—Applying Effects

The `gwt-widget` library is a terrific group of extensions and enhancements to the GWT framework maintained by Robert Hanson (`http://gwt-widget.sourceforge.net/`). It provides a Java class that wraps the effects, and we will use this class in our application. We will add a grid with two rows and four columns, each containing a small image file, and apply one effect to each of the images.

We need to reference the `gwt-widgets` module that provides the Java wrapper for the library. This is leveraging the module inheritance feature of GWT. We will go into an explanation of this concept in the *What Just happened?* section of this sample. Follow the steps given below to add the grid:

1. Add the following entry to the existing `Samples.gwt.xml` file in the `com.packtpub.gwtbook.samples` package:

    ```
    <inherits name='org.gwtwidgets.WidgetLibrary'/>
    ```

2. Add the prototype and `Script.aculo.us` JavaScript files that are used by the above module:

    ```
    <script type="text/JavaScript"src="JavaScript/prototype.js">
    </script>
    <script type="text/JavaScript" src="JavaScript/Scriptaculous.js">
    </script>
    ```

3. Create the user interface for this application in a new Java file named `ScriptaculousEffectsPanel.java` in the `com.packtpub.gwtbook.samples.client.panels` package. Create a grid with two rows and four columns. Create eight images, and eight buttons, and a work panel.

    ```
    private HorizontalPanel workPanel = new HorizontalPanel();
    private Grid grid = new Grid(2, 4);
    private Image packtlogo1 = new Image("images/packtlogo.jpg");
    private Image packtlogo2 = new Image("images/packtlogo.jpg");
    private Image packtlogo3 = new Image("images/packtlogo.jpg");
    private Image packtlogo4 = new Image("images/packtlogo.jpg");
    private Image packtlogo5 = new Image("images/packtlogo.jpg");
    private Image packtlogo6 = new Image("images/packtlogo.jpg");
    private Image packtlogo7 = new Image("images/packtlogo.jpg");
    ```

```
private Image packtlogo8 = new Image("images/packtlogo.jpg");
private Button fadeButton = new Button("fade");
private Button puffButton = new Button("puff");
private Button shakeButton = new Button("shake");
private Button growButton = new Button("grow");
private Button shrinkButton = new Button("shrink");
private Button pulsateButton = new Button("pulsate");
private Button blindUpButton = new Button("blindup");
private Button blindDownButton = new Button("blinddown");
```

4. Add the button and image for the fade effect to a VerticalPanel and add the panel to the grid.

```
VerticalPanel gridCellPanel = new VerticalPanel();
gridCellPanel.add(packtlogo1);
gridCellPanel.add(fadeButton);
grid.setWidget(0, 0, gridCellPanel);
```

5. Add an event handler for listening to the click on the fade effect button, and call the appropriate Script.aculo.us effect.

```
fadeButton.addClickListener(new ClickListener()
                           {
                             public void onClick(Widget sender)
                             {
                               Effect.fade(packtlogo1);
                             }
                           });
```

6. Add the button and image for the shake effect to a VerticalPanel and add the panel to the grid.

```
gridCellPanel = new VerticalPanel();
gridCellPanel.add(packtlogo3);
gridCellPanel.add(shakeButton);
grid.setWidget(0, 1, gridCellPanel);
```

7. Add an event handler for listening to the click on the shake effect button, and call the appropriate Script.aculo.us effect.

```
shakeButton.addClickListener(new ClickListener()
                            {
                              public void onClick(Widget sender)
                              {
                                Effect.shake(packtlogo3);
                              }
                            });
```

8. Add the button and image for the grow effect to a `VerticalPanel` and add the panel to the grid.

```
gridCellPanel = new VerticalPanel();
gridCellPanel.add(packtlogo4);
gridCellPanel.add(growButton);
grid.setWidget(0, 2, gridCellPanel);
```

9. Add an event handler for listening to the click on the grow effect button, and call the appropriate `Script.aculo.us` effect.

```
growButton.addClickListener(new ClickListener()
                            {
                                public void onClick(Widget sender)
                                {
                                    Effect.grow(packtlogo4);
                                }
                            });
```

10. Add the button and image for the blind up effect to a `VerticalPanel` and add the panel to the grid.

```
gridCellPanel = new VerticalPanel();
gridCellPanel.add(packtlogo8);
gridCellPanel.add(blindUpButton);
grid.setWidget(0, 3, gridCellPanel);
```

11. Add an event handler for listening to the click on the blind up effect button, and call the appropriate `Script.aculo.us` effect.

```
blindUpButton.addClickListener(new ClickListener()
                               {
                                   public void onClick(Widget sender)
                                   {
                                       Effect.blindUp(packtlogo8);
                                   }
                               });
```

12. Add the button and image for the puff effect to a `VerticalPanel` and add the panel to the grid.

```
gridCellPanel = new VerticalPanel();
gridCellPanel.add(packtlogo2);
gridCellPanel.add(puffButton);
grid.setWidget(1, 0, gridCellPanel);
```

13. Add an event handler for listening to the click on the puff effect button, and call the appropriate Script.aculo.us effect.

```
puffButton.addClickListener(new ClickListener()
                           {
                             public void onClick(Widget sender)
                             {
                               Effect.puff(packtlogo2);
                             }
                           });
```

14. Add the button and image for the shrink effect to a VerticalPanel and add the panel to the grid.

```
gridCellPanel = new VerticalPanel();
gridCellPanel.add(packtlogo5);
gridCellPanel.add(shrinkButton);
grid.setWidget(1, 1, gridCellPanel);
```

15. Add an event handler for listening to the click on the shrink effect button, and call the appropriate Script.aculo.us effect.

```
shrinkButton.addClickListener(new ClickListener()
                             {
                               public void onClick(Widget sender)
                               {
                                 Effect.shrink(packtlogo5);
                               }
                             });
```

16. Add the button and image for the pulsate effect to a VerticalPanel and add the panel to the grid.

```
gridCellPanel = new VerticalPanel();
gridCellPanel.add(packtlogo6);
gridCellPanel.add(pulsateButton);
grid.setWidget(1, 2, gridCellPanel);
```

17. Add an event handler for listening to the click on the pulsate effect button, and call the appropriate Script.aculo.us effect.

```
pulsateButton.addClickListener(new ClickListener()
                              {
                                public void onClick(Widget sender)
                                {
                                  Effect.pulsate(packtlogo6);
                                }
                              });
```

18. Finally, create a little info panel that displays descriptive text about this application, so that we can display this text when this sample is selected in the list of available samples in our `Samples` application. Add the info panel and the work panel to a dock panel, and initialize the widget.

```
HorizontalPanel infoPanel =
                          new HorizontalPanel();infoPanel.add
                  (new HTML("<div class='infoProse'>
                          Use nifty scriptaculous effects
                                   in GWT applications.
                                      </div>"));
workPanel.setStyleName("scriptaculouspanel");
workPanel.add(grid);
DockPanel workPane = new DockPanel();
workPane.add(infoPanel, DockPanel.NORTH);
workPane.add(workPanel, DockPanel.CENTER);
workPane.setCellHeight(workPanel, "100%");
workPane.setCellWidth(workPanel, "100%");
initWidget(workPane);
```

19. Add the `gwt-widgets.jar` to the buildpath in Eclipse so it can find the referenced classes.

Here are the various effects that we have in this application:

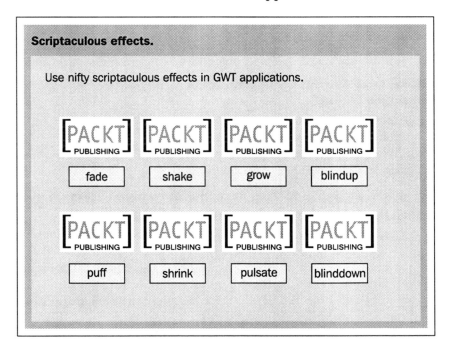

Click on each button to see the respective effect applied to the image.

What Just Happened?

Modules are XML files that contain the configuration settings for a GWT project. We have already seen and used the one for our `Samples` project. This is the file where we have referenced the external JavaScript files used by our application, along with entries for the RPC services used by our application, etc. GWT modules also have the ability to inherit from other modules. This enables the inheriting module to use resources that are declared in the inherited module. It prevents the issue of duplicate resource mapping and promotes reuse, making it easy to package GWT libraries as modules and distribute them and reuse them across projects. We can specify the module to be inherited from, by using the `inherits` tag and providing the fully qualified name of the module. All GWT applications must inherit from the `com.google.gwt.user.User` module, which provides the core web toolkit items. In this example we inherit from the `org.gwtwidgets.WidgetLibrary` that provides the `Script.aculo.us` effects class that we used in our application. Here is how we defined this inheritance in the `Samples.gwt.xml` file:

```
<inherits name='org.gwtwidgets.WidgetLibrary'/>
```

The `Script.aculo.us` effects are divided into two different types—Core effects and Combination effects. The core effects are the foundation of the library and the combination effects mix and use the core effects to create combination effects. The core effects in this library are:

- **Opacity**: Sets the transparency of an element.
- **Scale**: Scales an element smoothly.
- **Move By**: Moves an element by the given amount of pixels.
- **Highlight**: Draws attention to an element by changing its background color and flashing it.
- **Parallel**: Multiple effects are applied in parallel to the element.

The above core effects are mixed together to create the following combination effects:

- **Fade**: Fades an element away.
- **Puff**: Makes an element disappear in a cloud of smoke.
- **Shake**: Moves an element repeatedly to the left and right.
- **Blind Down**: Simulates a window blind coming down over an element.
- **Blind Up**: Simulates a window blind going up over an element.
- **Pulsate**: Fades an element in and out and makes it appear to be pulsating.
- **Grow**: Grows an element in size.
- **Shrink**: Reduces an element in size.

- **Squish**: Reduces an element by shrinking it to its left.
- **Fold**: First reduces an element to its top, then to its left, and eventually makes it disappear.

We position an image and a button inside each grid cell. When the button is clicked, we apply an effect to the image element that is above the button. We invoke an effect by providing the widget object to the desired effect method in the `org.gwtwidgets.client.wrap.Effect` class. All the methods in this class are static and each `Script.aculo.us` effect has a correspondingly named method in this class. So in order to fade an element, we call the `Effect.fade()` method and provide it with the image widget to which to apply the effect. These transitions are a very nice way to add dazzle to our application and provide a better user experience. You can also mix and match the provided effects in different ways to create and use customized effects.

Summary

We have covered several JavaScript libraries and their use in GWT applications. A very important thing to be aware of while using all these libraries is that including a lot of JavaScript will increase the bloat that has to be loaded by the browser and will almost certainly increase page load times, and make things run slower. So use the visual effects sparingly and do not go overboard with them. Another caveat is the lack of portability when using JSNI for your application. This can cause your application to work quite differently in different versions of browsers.

In this chapter we have learned about JSNI. We utilized JSNI to wrap the `Moo.fx` library and used its effects. We also wrapped different pieces of the `Rico` library and utilized it to create rounded corners for labels and a color selector application. We used the `Script.aculo.us` effects provided by the `gwt-widgets` library. We used an existing library in this case to provide the effects. We also learned how to use module inheritance in GWT.

In the next chapter, we are going to learn how to create custom GWT widgets that can be shared across projects.

7
Custom Widgets

GWT provides a wide variety of widgets—such as labels, text boxes, trees, etc., out of the box for you to use in your applications. These widgets provide a good starting point for building user interfaces, but will almost always not provide you with everything you need. This is where the concept of creating custom widgets by either combining the existing ones in newer and innovative ways, or writing new widgets from scratch comes in handy. In this chapter, we are going to tackle two things commonly used in web pages—a calendar display and a weather conditions display. Since these two functions are not provided by anything currently shipped in GWT, we will create these two widgets. We will also learn how to package them so that we can reuse them on a different GWT project if necessary.

The tasks that we will address are:

- Calendar widget
- Weather widget

Calendar Widget

We will create a reusable calendar widget, which can be easily used in multiple GWT applications. This widget is based on Alexei Sokolov's simple calendar widget (`http://gwt.components.googlepages.com/calendar`). We will adapt it to suit our requirements. The calendar will display the current date along with a listing for the current month and will enable navigation either forward or backward through the calendar. We will also provide a way to get back to the current day, no matter where we have navigated in the calendar.

Time for Action—Creating a Calendar

We will now create a calendar widget. The steps are as follows:

1. Create a new widget project to contain the artifacts for our custom
    widgets. We will create our widget in this project and then use it inside an
    application in our original Samples project. When we create the new project,
    the Widgets.gwt.xml file will be automatically created for us, and by default
    it will contain the following entry for inheriting from the User module. This
    is the one module that every GWT module needs to inherit from:

    ```
    <inherits name='com.google.gwt.user.User'/>
    ```

2. Create a new Java file named CalendarWidget.java in the com.packtpub.
    gwtbook.widgets.client package that extends the com.google.gwt.user.
    client.ui.Composite class and implements the com.google.gwt.user.
    client.ui.ClickListener interface:

    ```
    public class CalendarWidget extends Composite implements
    ClickListener
    {
    }
    ```

3. Create the elements needed for creating a navigation bar to go forward and
    backward in the calendar, along with a DockPanel class that will be the
    container for the calendar itself:

    ```
    private DockPanel navigationBar = new DockPanel();
    private Button previousMonth = new Button("&lt;", this);
    private Button nextMonth = new Button("&gt;", this);
    private final DockPanel outerDockPanel = new DockPanel();
    ```

4. Create string arrays to store the weekday names and the names of the
    months in a year. We will retrieve the names from these arrays to display in
    the user interface:

    ```
    private String[] daysInWeek = new String[] { "Sunday",
      "Monday", "Tuesday","Wednesday", "Thursday", "Friday",
                                            "Saturday"};
    private String[] monthsInYear = new String[] { "January",
        "February", "March", "April", "May", "June", "July",
        "August", "September", "October", "November", "December"};
    ```

5. Create a variable for holding the HTML used to display the title of the calendar. Create labels for displaying the week day and the date for the current day. Also, create and initialize a private variable that contains the current date:

```
private HTML calendarTitle = new HTML();
private Label dayOfWeek = new Label("");
private Label dateOfWeek = new Label("");
private Date currentDate = new Date();
```

6. Create a new `Grid` object that overrides the `clearCell()` method to set the text for the column cell:

```
private final Grid calendarGrid = new Grid(7, 7)
{
  public boolean clearCell(int row, int column)
  {
    boolean retValue = super.clearCell(row, column);
    Element td = getCellFormatter().getElement(row, column);
    DOM.setInnerHTML(td, "");
    return retValue;
  }
};
```

7. Create a private static class named `CalendarCell` that extends the HTML class:

```
private static class CalendarCell extends HTML
{
  private int day;
  public CalendarCell(String cellText, int day)
  {
    super(cellText);
    this.day = day;
  }
  public int getDay()
  {
    return day;
  }
}
```

An instance of this class will be added to the `grid` object we created earlier, to display a single calendar element in a cell.

8. Add accessors to the `CalendarWidget` class for getting the current date, along with the day, month, and year components of the current date:

```
public int getYear()
{
```

```
      return 1900 + currentDate.getYear();
    }
    public int getMonth()
    {
      return currentDate.getMonth();
    }
    public int getDay()
    {
      return currentDate.getDate();
    }
    public Date getDate()
    {
      return currentDate;
    }
```

These methods will be used to retrieve the individual data for a given calendar date.

9. Add mutators to the `CalendarWidget` class for modifying the day, month, and year components of the `currentDate` variable:

```
    private void setDate(int year, int month, int day)
    {
      currentDate = new Date(year - 1900, month, day);
    }
    private void setYear(int year)
    {
      currentDate.setYear(year - 1900);
    }
    private void setMonth(int month)
    {
      currentDate.setMonth(month);
    }
```

10. Create a method for computing the calendar for a month previous to the current month:

```
    public void computeCalendarForPreviousMonth()
    {
      int month = getMonth() - 1;
      if (month < 0)
      {
        setDate(getYear() - 1, 11, getDay());
      }
      else
      {
        setMonth(month);
      }
```

```
        renderCalendar();
    }
```

We will use this when the user clicks on the button for navigating to the previous month.

11. Create a method for computing the calendar for a month after to the current month:

```
public void computeCalendarForNextMonth()
{
    int month = getMonth() + 1;
    if (month > 11)
    {
        setDate(getYear() + 1, 0, getDay());
    }
    else
    {
        setMonth(month);
    }
    renderCalendar();
}
```

We will use this when the user clicks on the button for navigating to the next month.

12. Create a method for computing the number of days in a given month. There is no simple method for getting this information currently; so we need to calculate it:

```
private int getDaysInMonth(int year, int month)
{
 switch (month)
 {
   case 1:
     if ((year % 4 == 0 && year % 100 != 0) || year % 400 == 0)
     return 29;
     else
     return 28;
   case 3:
     return 30;
   case 5:
     return 30;
   case 8:
     return 30;
   case 10:
     return 30;
```

```
        default:
          return 31;
    }
  }
```

13. Create a `renderCalendar()` method that can draw the calendar and all of its elements. Get the various components of the currently set `date` object, set the calendar title, and format the calendar grid. Also compute the number of days in the month and the current day, and set the date and weekday label values. Finally, set the values of the `grid` cells to the computed calendar values:

```
private void renderCalendar()
{
  int year = getYear();
  int month = getMonth();
  int day = getDay();
  calendarTitle.setText(monthsInYear[month] + " " + year);
  calendarGrid.getRowFormatter().setStyleName(0, "weekheader");
  for (int i = 0; i < daysInWeek.length; i++)
  {
    calendarGrid.getCellFormatter().setStyleName(0, i, "days");
    calendarGrid.setText(0, i, daysInWeek[i].substring(0, 1));
  }
  Date now = new Date();
  int sameDay = now.getDate();
  int today = (now.getMonth() == month && now.getYear() + 1900
               == year) ? sameDay : 0;
  int firstDay = new Date(year - 1900, month, 1).getDay();
  int numOfDays = getDaysInMonth(year, month);
  int weekDay = now.getDay();
  dayOfWeek.setText(daysInWeek[weekDay]);
  dateOfWeek.setText("" + day);
  int j = 0;
  for (int i = 1; i < 6; i++)
  {
    for (int k = 0; k < 7; k++, j++)
    {
      int displayNum = (j - firstDay + 1);
      if (j < firstDay || displayNum > numOfDays)
      {
        calendarGrid.getCellFormatter().setStyleName(i, k,
                                                    "empty");
        calendarGrid.setHTML(i, k, " ");
      }
```

```
        else
        {
          HTML html = new calendarCell("<span>"+
          String.valueOf(displayNum) + "</span>",displayNum);
          html.addClickListener(this);
          calendarGrid.getCellFormatter().setStyleName(i, k,
                                                      "cell");

          if (displayNum == today)
          {
            calendarGrid.getCellFormatter().addStyleName(i, k,
                                                      "today");
          }
          else if (displayNum == sameDay)
          {
            calendarGrid.getCellFormatter().addStyleName(i, k,
                                                      "day");
          }
          calendarGrid.setWidget(i, k, html);
        }
      }
    }
  }
```

14. Create the constructor `CalendarWidget()` to initialize and lay out all the various elements that compose our calendar widget:

```
HorizontalPanel hpanel = new HorizontalPanel();
navigationBar.setStyleName("navbar");
calendarTitle.setStyleName("header");
HorizontalPanel prevButtons = new HorizontalPanel();
prevButtons.add(previousMonth);
HorizontalPanel nextButtons = new HorizontalPanel();
nextButtons.add(nextMonth);
navigationBar.add(prevButtons, DockPanel.WEST);
navigationBar.setCellHorizontalAlignment(prevButtons,
 DockPanel.ALIGN_LEFT);
navigationBar.add(nextButtons, DockPanel.EAST);
navigationBar.setCellHorizontalAlignment(nextButtons,
 DockPanel.ALIGN_RIGHT);
navigationBar.add(calendarTitle, DockPanel.CENTER);
navigationBar.setVerticalAlignment(DockPanel.ALIGN_MIDDLE);
navigationBar.setCellHorizontalAlignment(calendarTitle,
 HasAlignment.ALIGN_CENTER);
navigationBar.setCellVerticalAlignment(calendarTitle,
 HasAlignment.ALIGN_MIDDLE);
navigationBar.setCellWidth(calendarTitle, "100%");
```

15. In the constructor, round the container panel that will hold all of the widget elements using the `Rico` class that we created in Chapter 6. As we learned in Chapter 6, the `Rico` class has static methods that can be used to get access to the rounding method. We are directly using the `Rico` class created earlier to keep things simple, but another way would be to split off the `Rico`-related functionality into its own separate module and then use it here. Initialize the widget with this container panel:

```
initWidget(hpanel);
calendarGrid.setStyleName("table");
calendarGrid.setCellSpacing(0);
DOM.setAttribute(hpanel.getElement(), "id", "calDiv");
DOM.setAttribute(hpanel.getElement(), "className",
  "CalendarWidgetHolder");
Rico.corner(hpanel.getElement(), null);
hpanel.add(outerDockPanel);
```

16. Also, in the constructor add the navigation bar, the calendar grid, and the **today** button to the vertical panel:

```
VerticalPanel calendarPanel = new VerticalPanel();
calendarPanel.add(navigationBar);
VerticalPanel vpanel = new VerticalPanel();
calendarPanel.add(calendarGrid);
calendarPanel.add(todayButton);
```

17. Register an event handler to listen for clicks on the **today** button, and to redraw the calendar to the current date:

```
todayButton.setStyleName("todayButton");
todayButton.addClickListener(new ClickListener()
{
  public void onClick(Widget sender)
  {
    currentDate = new Date();
    renderCalendar();
  }
});
```

18. Add the styles for the day and weekday labels and add the widgets to the vertical panel:

```
dayOfWeek.setStyleName("dayOfWeek");
dateOfWeek.setStyleName("dateOfWeek");
vpanel.add(dayOfWeek);
vpanel.add(dateOfWeek);
```

19. Add the two panels to the main panel for the widget:

```
outerDockPanel.add(vpanel, DockPanel.CENTER);
outerDockPanel.add(calendarPanel, DockPanel.EAST);
```

20. Draw the calendar and also register to sink all click events:

```
renderCalendar();
setStyleName("CalendarWidget");
this.sinkEvents(Event.ONCLICK);
```

21. Create a JAR file that contains the widget that we have created. You can export a JAR file by using the JAR Packager tool built into Eclipse. Select **Export** from the **File** menu and you will have a similar screen to this:

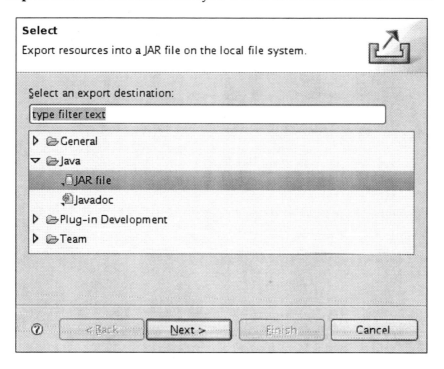

22. Fill in the information, as it appears in the next screenshot, for creating the JAR, and select the resources that will be included in it:

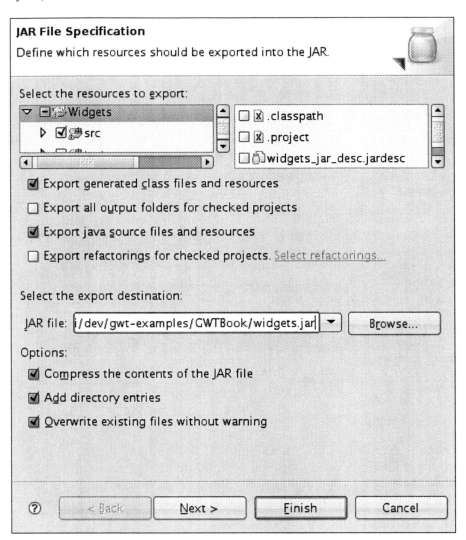

23. Create the JAR file and save as `widgets_jar_desc.jardesc`, so that we can recreate the JAR easily whenever we need to. This is shown in the following screenshot:

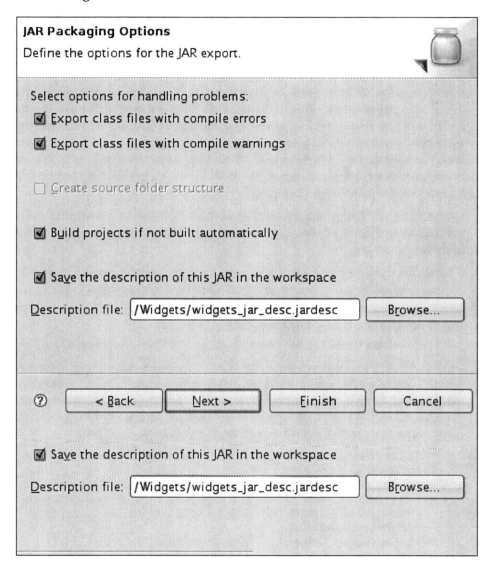

24. Now that we have successfully created the JAR file named `widgets.jar` that contains our calendar widget, let us actually use it in a different project. Add this JAR to the `buildpath` for our `Samples` Eclipse project, so that the classes we need can be found on the `classpath` for the project.

25. We also need to add the `widgets.jar` file to the scripts for running in hosted mode and web mode. Modify the `Samples-shell.cmd` file and the `Samples-compile.cmd` file to add the path to this JAR file.

26. Modify the module XML file for the `Samples` project—`Samples.gwt.xml`—to inherit from the widgets module. Add the following entry to the file:

```
<inherits name='com.packtpub.gwtbook.widgets.Widgets'/>
```

   This entry is an indicator to the GWT framework that the current module will use resources from the `com.packtpub.gwtbook.widgets.Widgets` module. GWT also provides an automatic resource injection mechanism to automatically load resources used by a module. This is accomplished by creating the modules with references to the external JavaScript and CSS files used by the module, and is particularly useful when you create reusable modules, and want to ensure that the users of the module have access to the particular stylesheets or JavaScript files used by the module.

   In our case, we can probably rewrite and split off our `Rico` support, which we added in Chapter 6, into its own module, but for the sake of simplicity we are using it as it is.

27. Create the user interface for the calendar widget application in a new Java file named `CalendarWidgetPanel.java` in the `com.packtpub.gwtbook.samples.client.panels` package in the `Samples` project. Create a work panel for holding the calendar sample:

```
private VerticalPanel workPanel = new VerticalPanel();
```

28. In the constructor, create a new class `CalendarWidget` and add it to the panel. Create a little info panel that displays descriptive text about this application, so that we can display the text when this sample is selected in the list of available samples in our `Samples` application. Add the info panel and the work panel to a dock panel, and initialize the widget:

```
HorizontalPanel infoPanel = new HorizontalPanel();
infoPanel.add(new HTML
  ("<div class='infoProse'>Click on the navigation buttons to
     go forward and backward through the calendar. When you
     want to come back to todays date, click on the Today
     button.</div>"));
CalendarWidget calendar = new CalendarWidget();
workPanel.add(calendar);
DockPanel workPane = new DockPanel();
workPane.add(infoPanel, DockPanel.NORTH);
workPane.add(workPanel, DockPanel.CENTER);
workPane.setCellHeight(workPanel, "100%");
workPane.setCellWidth(workPanel, "100%");
initWidget(workPane);
```

Run the application to see the calendar widget in action:

What Just Happened?

A custom widget encapsulates functionality and enables reuse across multiple projects. There are three ways to create a custom GWT widget:

- **Composite**: Composite is a special GWT class that is itself a widget, and can act as a container for other widgets. This lets us easily compose a complex widget comprising any number of components.

- **Java**: Create a widget from scratch similar to the way all the basic widgets of GWT, such as Button are written.

- **JavaScript**: Implement a widget whose methods call JavaScript. This method should be chosen carefully, as the code will need to be written to carefully consider the cross-browser implications.

Normal GWT widgets are just wrappers around HTML elements. A composite widget is a complex widget composed of several simple widgets. It controls the methods that are publicly accessible to the clients of the widget. You can, thus, expose only the events that you want. Composite is the simplest and quickest way to build a widget. In this example, we create a calendar widget by extending the

`Composite` class, and adding various components to it. The calendar consists of two main panels—the one on the left displays the weekday and the actual date, while the panel on the right displays the actual calendar along with the buttons for navigating forward and backward through the calendar. You can use these buttons to go to a different date. Anytime you want to return to the calendar for today's date, click on the **Today** button, and the calendar will again be rendered for the current date.

We created a container named `HorizontalPanel` that contains the various components of the calendar widget. This panel is given a nice rounded corner effect by using the `Rico` library that we created in the previous chapter.

```
DOM.setAttribute(hpanel.getElement(), "id", "calDiv");
DOM.setAttribute(hpanel.getElement(), "className",
                                      "CalendarWidgetHolder");
Rico.corner(hpanel.getElement(), null);
```

For the calendar, we used a `Grid` object with seven rows and seven columns. We overrode its `clearCell()` method to clear the contents of the cell by setting the text for the TD element to an empty string:

```
public boolean clearCell(int row, int column)
{
  boolean retValue = super.clearCell(row, column);
  Element td = getCellFormatter().getElement(row, column);
  DOM.setInnerHTML(td, "");
  return retValue;
}
```

This grid was created by populating each of its cells with `CalendarCell`. This is a custom class that we created where each of the cells can take an HTML snippet as the text, and lets us lay out a much better grid.

```
private static class calendarCell extends HTML
{
  private int day;
  public calendarCell(String cellText, int day)
  {
    super(cellText);
    this.day = day;
  }
  public int getDay()
  {
    return day;
  }
}
```

The renderCalendar() method does the bulk of the work in this widget. It sets the values for the weekday and the date, and also draws the calendar itself. When we create the calendar grid, we set the styles for each individual cell. If the cell happens to be the current date, we set it to a different style; so visually we can immediately discern the current date by just looking at the grid. When the calendar widget is initialized, it automatically draws the calendar for the current date. The navigation bar contains two buttons—one for navigating forward to go to the next month, and the other button for navigating backward to the previous month. When one of the two navigation buttons is clicked, we redraw the calendar. So, for instance, when we click on the previous button, we compute the previous month and redraw the calendar:

```
public void computeCalendarForPreviousMonth()
{
  int month = getMonth() - 1;
  if (month < 0)
  {
    setDate(getYear() - 1, 11, getDay());
  }
  else
  {
    setMonth(month);
  }
  renderCalendar();
}
```

We also added a button to the calendar so as to let us redraw the calendar to the current date. After navigating either forward or backward in the calendar, we can click on the **Today** button, and have the calendar rendered for the current date:

```
todayButton.addClickListener(new ClickListener()
{
  public void onClick(Widget sender)
  {
    currentDate = new Date();
    renderCalendar();
  }
});
```

We utilized the built-in functionality in Eclipse to export our widget resources as a JAR file. This JAR file can be shared among teams or projects, and reused. We used this exported widgets.jar file in our Samples project, by creating a simple panel, instantiating the calendar widget, and adding it to the panel. The file also needs to be added to the compile and shell batch files for the project; so that it can be found on the classpath when either of these commands is run. We could have done some of the date manipulation in a simpler way by using the Calendar class that is available in the JDK 1.4 + versions. However, we could not use the `Calendar` class as it is not one of the JRE classes that are provided by the GWT framework currently. So if we would have used it, we had had compilation errors. If in the future this class is supported by GWT, it should be quite simple to switch it out to use the functionality provided by the `Calendar` class to perform some of the date manipulation.

Weather Widget

We will create a weather widget that uses the Yahoo Weather RSS service to retrieve the weather information and display the current weather conditions. We will create an RPC service that provides this functionality, and then use the RPC in our widget to display the weather information for a given US ZIP code. The user interface for this widget will contain an image for the current weather condition, along with all the other weather-related information that is available via the Yahoo weather service.

Time for Action—Creating a Weather Information Service

This widget will also be created in the same widgets project that we used to create the calendar widget in the previous section. The steps are as follows:

1. Create a new Java file named `Weather.java` in the `com.packtpub.gwtbook.widgets.client` package. This class will encapsulate all the weather-related information for a given ZIP code, and will be used as the return parameter in the RPC service that we will create later on in this example. We can also use the recently added GWT support for client-side XML parsing to read an XML string returned to the client. We are going to learn about GWT's XML support in Chapter 9. For now, we are going to use a simple object to encapsulate the returned weather information. This will enable us to focus on the custom widget functionality and keeps things simple. Create variables for each of the properties:

```
private String zipCode = "";
private String chill = "";
private String direction = "";
private String speed = "";
private String humidity = "";
private String visibility = "";
private String pressure = "";
private String rising = "";
private String sunrise = "";
private String sunset = "";
```

```
private String latitude = "";
private String longitude = "";
private String currentCondition = "";
private String currentTemp = "";
private String imageUrl = "";
private String city = "";
private String state = "";
private String error = "";
```

2. Add methods for getting and setting the various weather-related properties for this class. Here are the methods to get and set chill, city, current condition, and current temperature:

```
public String getChill()
{
  return chill;
}
public void setChill(String chill)
{
  this.chill = chill;
}
public String getCity()
{
  return city;
}
public void setCity(String city)
{
  this.city = city;
}
public String getCurrentCondition()
{
  return currentCondition;
}
public void setCurrentCondition(String currentCondition)
{
  this.currentCondition = currentCondition;
}
public String getCurrentTemp()
{
  return currentTemp;
}
public void setCurrentTemp(String currentTemp)
{
  this.currentTemp = currentTemp;
}
```

3. Add methods to get and set direction, error, humidity, and image URL:

```
public String getDirection()
{
  return direction;
}
public void setDirection(String direction)
{
  this.direction = direction;
}
public String getError()
{
  return error;
}
public void setError(String error)
{
  this.error = error;
}
public String getHumidity()
{
return humidity;
}
public void setHumidity(String humidity)
{
  this.humidity = humidity;
}
public String getImageUrl()
{
  return imageUrl;
}
public void setImageUrl(String imageUrl)
{
  this.imageUrl = imageUrl;
}
```

4. Add methods to get and set latitude, longitude, pressure, and barometer rising:

```
public String getLatitude()
{
  return latitude;
}
public void setLatitude(String latitude)
{
  this.latitude = latitude;
}
```

```
public String getLongitude()
{
  return longitude;
}
public void setLongitude(String longitude)
{
  this.longitude = longitude;
}
public String getPressure()
{
  return pressure;
}
public void setPressure(String pressure)
{
  this.pressure = pressure;
}
public String getRising()
{
  return rising;
}
public void setRising(String rising)
{
  this.rising = rising;
}
```

5. Add methods to get and set speed, state, sunrise, and sunset values:

```
public String getSpeed()
{
  return speed;
}
public void setSpeed(String speed)
{
  this.speed = speed;
}
public String getState()
{
  return state;
}
public void setState(String state)
{
  this.state = state;
}
public String getSunrise()
{
```

```
        return sunrise;
      }
      public void setSunrise(String sunrise)
      {
        this.sunrise = sunrise;
      }
      public String getSunset()
      {
        return sunset;
      }
      public void setSunset(String sunset)
      {
        this.sunset = sunset;
      }
```

6. Add methods to get and set the visibility and the ZIP code:

```
      public String getVisibility()
      {
        return visibility;
      }
      public void setVisibility(String visibility)
      {
        this.visibility = visibility;
      }
      public String getZipCode()
      {
        return zipCode;
      }
      public void setZipCode(String zipCode)
      {
        this.zipCode = zipCode;
      }
```

7. Create the Weather() constructor to create a weather object:

```
      public Weather(String zipCode, String chill, String direction,
        String speed, String humidity, String visibility, String
        pressure, String rising, String sunrise, String sunset,
        String latitude, String longitude, String currentCondition,
        String currentTemp, String imageUrl, String city, String
        state)
      {
        this.zipCode = zipCode;
        this.chill = chill;
        this.direction = direction;
```

```
        this.speed = speed;
        this.humidity = humidity;
        this.visibility = visibility;
        this.pressure = pressure;
        this.rising = rising;
        this.sunrise = sunrise;
        this.sunset = sunset;
        this.latitude = latitude;
        this.longitude = longitude;
        this.currentCondition = currentCondition;
        this.currentTemp = currentTemp;
        this.imageUrl = imageUrl;
        this.city = city;
        this.state = state;
    }
```

8. Create a new Java file named `WeatherService.java` in the `com.packtpub.gwtbook.widgets.client` package. This is the service definition for the weather service. Define one method to retrieve the weather data by providing a ZIP code:

```
public interface WeatherService extends RemoteService
{
    public Weather getWeather(String zipCode);
}
```

9. Create the asynchronous version of this service definition interface in a new Java file named `WeatherServiceAsync.java` in the `com.packtpub.gwtbook.widgets.client` package:

```
public interface WeatherServiceAsync
{
    public void getWeather(String zipCode, AsyncCallback
                                               callback);
}
```

10. Create the implementation of the weather service in a new Java file named `WeatherServiceImpl.java` in the `com.packtpub.gwtbook.widgets.server` package. We are going to use two third-party libraries from the Dom4j (`http://www.dom4j.org/`) and Jaxen (`http://jaxen.codehaus.org/`) projects in this sample, to make it easier for us to parse the Yahoo RSS feed. Download the current versions of these libraries to the `lib` folder. Add `dom4j-xxx.jar` and `jaxen-xxx.jar` in the `lib` folder to the `buildpath` for Eclipse. Add the necessary code to retrieve the weather data for a given ZIP code by accessing the Yahoo Weather RSS service in the `getWeather()` method.

Create a SAX parser first:

```
public Weather getWeather(String zipCode)
{
  SAXReader reader = new SAXReader();
  Weather weather = new Weather();
  Document document;
}
```

11. Retrieve the RSS document for the provided ZIP code:

```
try
{
  document = reader.read(new URL
    ("http://xml.weather.yahoo.com/forecastrss?p=" + z ipCode));
}
catch (MalformedURLException e)
{
  e.printStackTrace();
}
catch (DocumentException e)
{
  e.printStackTrace();
}
```

12. Create a new XPath expression and add the namespaces that we are interested in to the expression:

```
XPath expression = new Dom4jXPath("/rss/channel");
expression.addNamespace("yweather",
  "http://xml.weather.yahoo.com/ns/rss/1.0");
expression.addNamespace("geo",
  "http://www.w3.org/2003/01/geo/wgs84_pos#");
```

We will later on use this expression to access the data we need from the document.

13. Select the root node in the retrieved XML document, and check for any errors. Return a `weather` object with an error message set, if any errors are found in the XML:

```
Node result = (Node) expression.selectSingleNode(document);
String error = result.valueOf("/rss/channel/description");
if (error.equals("Yahoo! Weather Error"))
{
  weather.setError("Invalid zipcode "+ zipCode+
    " provided. No weather information available for this
                                            location.");
  return weather;
}
```

14. Select the description section using XPath, and then parse it to determine the URL for the image that pertains to the returned weather data. Set this information in the `ImageUrl` property of the `weather` object:

```
String descriptionSection = result.valueOf
   ("/rss/channel/item/description");
weather.setImageUrl(descriptionSection.substring
   (descriptionSection.indexOf("src=") + 5,
    descriptionSection.indexOf(".gif") + 4));
```

15. Use XPath expressions to select all the data that we are interested in from the XML document, and set the various properties of the `weather` object. Finally, return the object as the return value from our service:

```
weather.setCity(result.valueOf("//yweather:location/@city"));
weather.setState(result.valueOf
   ("//yweather:location/@region"));
weather.setChill(result.valueOf("//yweather:wind/@chill"));
weather.setDirection(result.valueOf
   ("//yweather:wind/@direction"));
weather.setSpeed(result.valueOf("//yweather:wind/@speed"));
weather.setHumidity(result.valueOf
   ("//yweather:atmosphere/@humidity"));
weather.setVisibility(result.valueOf
   ("//yweather:atmosphere/@visibility"));
weather.setPressure(result.valueOf
   ("//yweather:atmosphere/@pressure"));
weather.setRising(result.valueOf
   ("//yweather:atmosphere/@rising"));
weather.setSunrise(result.valueOf
   ("//yweather:astronomy/@sunrise"));
weather.setSunset(result.valueOf
   ("//yweather:astronomy/@sunset"));
weather.setCurrentCondition(result.valueOf
   ("//yweather:condition/@text"));
weather.setCurrentTemp(result.valueOf
   ("//yweather:condition/@temp"));
weather.setLatitude(result.valueOf("//geo:lat"));
weather.setLongitude(result.valueOf("//geo:long"));
return weather;
```

16. Our server-side implementation is now complete. Create a new Java file named `WeatherWidget.java` in the `com.packtpub.gwtbook.widgets.client` package that extends the `com.google.gwt.user.client.ui.Composite` class and implements the `com.google.gwt.user.client.ui.ChangeListener` interface:

```
public class WeatherWidget extends Composite implements
  ChangeListener
{
}
```

17. In the `WeatherWidget` class, create panels for displaying the current weather image, conditions, along with atmospheric, wind, astronomical, and geographic measurements:

```
private VerticalPanel imagePanel = new VerticalPanel();
private HorizontalPanel tempPanel = new HorizontalPanel();
private VerticalPanel tempHolderPanel = new VerticalPanel();
private HorizontalPanel currentPanel = new HorizontalPanel();
private HorizontalPanel windPanel = new HorizontalPanel();
private HorizontalPanel windPanel2 = new HorizontalPanel();
private HorizontalPanel atmospherePanel = new
  HorizontalPanel();
private HorizontalPanel atmospherePanel2 = new
  HorizontalPanel();
private HorizontalPanel astronomyPanel = new HorizontalPanel();
private HorizontalPanel geoPanel = new HorizontalPanel();
private Image image = new Image();
private Label currentTemp = new Label("");
private Label currentCondition = new Label("");
```

18. Create labels for displaying all of this information, along with a textbox to allow users to enter the ZIP code of the place whose weather is to be displayed in the widget:

```
private Label windChill = new Label("");
private Label windDirection = new Label("");
private Label windSpeed = new Label("");
private Label atmHumidity = new Label("");
private Label atmVisibility = new Label("");
private Label atmpressure = new Label("");
private Label atmRising = new Label("");
private Label astSunrise = new Label("");
private Label astSunset = new Label("");
private Label latitude = new Label("");
private Label longitude = new Label("");
private Label windLabel = new Label("Wind");
private Label astLabel = new Label("Astronomy");
private Label atmLabel = new Label("Atmosphere");
private Label geoLabel = new Label("Geography");
private Label cityLabel = new Label("");
private TextBox zipCodeInput = new TextBox();
```

19. Create and initialize the `WeatherService` object and set the entry-point URL for the weather service:

```
final WeatherServiceAsync weatherService =
   (WeatherServiceAsync) GWT.create(WeatherService.class);
ServiceDefTarget endpoint = (ServiceDefTarget) weatherService;
endpoint.setServiceEntryPoint(GWT.getModuleBaseURL() +
                                          "weather");
```

20. Create the `WeatherWidget()` constructor. In the constructor, create the work panel; initialize the widget with our main panel and register to receive all change events:

```
VerticalPanel workPanel = new VerticalPanel();
initWidget(workPanel);
this.sinkEvents(Event.ONCHANGE);
```

21. Set `id` for the work panel, and use the `Rico` library, as in the previous example, to round the corner for the panel:

```
DOM.setAttribute(workPanel.getElement(), "id", "weatherDiv");
DOM.setAttribute(workPanel.getElement(), "className",
                                          "weatherHolder");
Rico.corner(workPanel.getElement(), null);
```

22. Add the requisite styles for each element and add the element to the various panels:

```
image.setStyleName("weatherImage");
imagePanel.add(image);
currentCondition.setStyleName("currentCondition");
imagePanel.add(currentCondition);
currentPanel.add(imagePanel);
currentTemp.setStyleName("currentTemp");
tempPanel.add(currentTemp);
tempPanel.add(new HTML("<div class='degrees'>&deg;</div>"));
tempHolderPanel.add(tempPanel);
cityLabel.setStyleName("city");
tempHolderPanel.add(cityLabel);
currentPanel.add(tempHolderPanel);
windDirection.setStyleName("currentMeasurementsDegrees");
windChill.setStyleName("currentMeasurementsDegrees");
windSpeed.setStyleName("currentMeasurements");
windPanel.add(windDirection);
windPanel.add(new HTML
   ("<div class='measurementDegrees'>&deg;</div>"));
windPanel.add(windSpeed);
windPanel2.add(windChill);
```

```
windPanel2.add(new HTML
    ("<div class='measurementDegrees'>&deg;</div>"));
atmHumidity.setStyleName("currentMeasurements");
atmpressure.setStyleName("currentMeasurements");
atmVisibility.setStyleName("currentMeasurements");
atmRising.setStyleName("currentMeasurements");
atmospherePanel.add(atmHumidity);
atmospherePanel.add(atmVisibility);
atmospherePanel2.add(atmpressure);
astSunrise.setStyleName("currentMeasurements");
astSunset.setStyleName("currentMeasurements");
astronomyPanel.add(astSunrise);
astronomyPanel.add(astSunset);
latitude.setStyleName("currentMeasurements");
longitude.setStyleName("currentMeasurements");
geoPanel.add(latitude);
geoPanel.add(longitude);
windLabel.setStyleName("conditionPanel");
atmLabel.setStyleName("conditionPanel");
astLabel.setStyleName("conditionPanel");
geoLabel.setStyleName("conditionPanel");
```

23. Add all the panels to the main work panel:

```
workPanel.add(currentPanel);
workPanel.add(windLabel);
workPanel.add(windPanel);
workPanel.add(windPanel2);
workPanel.add(atmLabel);
workPanel.add(atmospherePanel);
workPanel.add(atmospherePanel2);
workPanel.add(astLabel);
workPanel.add(astronomyPanel);
workPanel.add(geoLabel);
workPanel.add(geoPanel);
```

24. Create a small panel for inputting the ZIP code and a buffer panel to separate it from the rest of the panels that compose this widget. Finally invoke the `getAndRenderWeather()` method to get the weather information. Create this method:

```
HorizontalPanel bufferPanel = new HorizontalPanel();
bufferPanel.add(new HTML("<div> </div>"));
HorizontalPanel zipCodeInputPanel = new HorizontalPanel();
Label zipCodeInputLabel = new Label("Enter Zip:");
zipCodeInputLabel.setStyleName("zipCodeLabel");
```

```
zipCodeInput.setStyleName("zipCodeInput");
zipCodeInput.setText("90210");
zipCodeInput.addChangeListener(this);
zipCodeInputPanel.add(zipCodeInputLabel);
zipCodeInputPanel.add(zipCodeInput);
workPanel.add(zipCodeInputPanel);
workPanel.add(bufferPanel);
getAndRenderWeather(zipCodeInput.getText());
```

25. Create a private method named `getAndRenderWeather()` for getting the weather information from the service and displaying it in our user interface:

```
private void getAndRenderWeather(String zipCode)
{
  AsyncCallback callback = new AsyncCallback()
  {
    public void onSuccess(Object result)
    {
      Weather weather = (Weather) result;
      if (weather.getError().length() > 0)
      {
        Window.alert(weather.getError());
        return;
      }
      image.setUrl(weather.getImageUrl());
      currentTemp.setText(weather.getCurrentTemp());
      currentCondition.setText(weather.getCurrentCondition());
      windDirection.setText("Direction : " +
                                        weather.getDirection());
      windChill.setText("Chill : " + weather.getChill());
      windSpeed.setText("Speed : " + weather.getSpeed() +
                                            " mph");
      atmHumidity.setText("Humidity : " + weather.getHumidity()
                                            + " %");
      atmpressure.setText("Barometer : "+ weather.getPressure()
                    + " in and "+ getBarometerState(
                    Integer.parseInt(weather.getRising())));
                    atmVisibility.setText("Visibility : "+
                    (Integer.parseInt(weather.getVisibility())
                    / 100) + " mi");
      astSunrise.setText("Sunrise : " + weather.getSunrise());
      astSunset.setText("Sunset : " + weather.getSunset());
      latitude.setText("Latitude : " + weather.getLatitude());
      longitude.setText("Longitude : " +
                                        weather.getLongitude());
      cityLabel.setText(weather.getCity() + ", " +
```

```
                      weather.getState());
              }
              public void onFailure(Throwable caught)
              {
                 Window.alert(caught.getMessage());
              }
        weatherService.getWeather(zipCode, callback);
```

26. Add a private method that returns the display text based on the integer value of the rising attribute:

```
private String getBarometerState(int rising)
{
  if (rising == 0)
  {
    return "steady";
  }
  else if (rising == 1)
  {
    return "rising";
  }
  else
  {
    return "falling";
  }
}
```

27. Add an event handler to get and render the new weather information when the user types in a new ZIP code in the textbox:

```
public void onChange(Widget sender)
{
  if (zipCodeInput.getText().length() == 5)
  {
    getAndRenderWeather(zipCodeInput.getText());
  }
}
```

28. Rebuild the `widgets.jar` file to contain the new weather widget. Now we can use our new JAR file to create a user interface that instantiates and uses this widget.

29. Create the user interface for the weather widget application in a new Java file named `WeatherWidgetPanel.java` in the `com.packtpub.gwtbook. samples.client.panels` package in the `Samples` project. Create a work panel for holding the weather widget:

    ```
    private VerticalPanel workPanel = new VerticalPanel();
    ```

30. In the constructor, create a new `WeatherWidget` and add it to the panel. Since we are already inheriting from the widgets module in the `Samples.gwt.xml` file, all the requisite classes should be resolved correctly. Create a little info panel that displays descriptive text about this application, so that we can display the text when this sample is selected in the list of available samples in our `Samples` application. Add the info panel and the work panel to a dock panel, and initialize the widget:

    ```
    HorizontalPanel infoPanel = new HorizontalPanel();
    infoPanel.add(new HTML
      ("<div class='infoProse'>A custom widget for viewing the
          weather conditions for a US city by entering the zipcode
          in the textbox.</div>"));:
    WeatherWidget weather = new WeatherWidget();
    workPanel.add(weather);
    DockPanel workPane = new DockPanel();
    workPane.add(infoPanel, DockPanel.NORTH);
    workPane.add(workPanel, DockPanel.CENTER);
    workPane.setCellHeight(workPanel, "100%");
    workPane.setCellWidth(workPanel, "100%");
    initWidget(workPane);
    ```

Here is a screenshot of the weather widget:

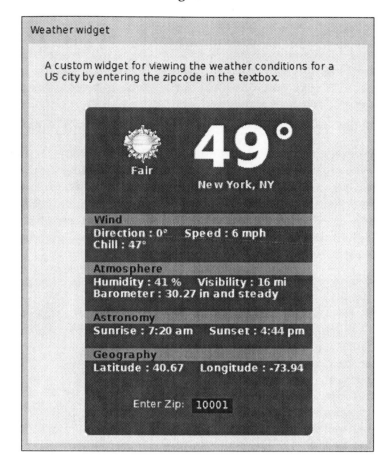

Type a new US ZIP code to see the weather conditions for that area.

What Just Happened?

Yahoo! Weather provides weather data and information for a provided US ZIP code via RSS. **Really Simple Syndication (RSS)** is a lightweight XML format that was primarily designed for distributing web content such as headlines. The service provided can be accessed via a URL-based format and by providing the ZIP code as a parameter to the URL. The response is an XML message that can be parsed and searched for the required data.

We create an RPC WeatherService that accesses the Yahoo service, parses the data, and provides it to us in the form of a simple weather object. This Weather class models the weather for a single ZIP code. Each instance of the Weather class contains the following attributes that are set by our WeatherService:

- `zipCode`: The ZIP code whose weather needs to be retrieved.

- `currentTemp`: The current temperature.

- `currentConditions`: The text that reflects the current weather conditions.

- `chill`: The wind chill for this location.

- `direction`: The wind direction.

- `speed`: The current wind speed for this location.

- `humidity`: The current humidity for this location.

- `visibility`: The current visibility.

- `pressure`: The current barometric pressure.

- `rising`: Indicator to inform if the barometric pressure is rising, falling, or steady.

- `sunrise`: Time of sunrise.

- `sunset`: Time of sunset.

- `latitude`: Latitude of this location.

- `longitude`: Longitude of this location.

- `city`: The city that corresponds to this ZIP code.

- `state`: The state that corresponds to this ZIP code.

- `imageUrl`: The URL for the image that represents the current weather conditions.

- `error`: If there is any error encountered while retrieving the weather information for a given ZIP code, this attribute is set. This enables the UI to display a message box with this error.

We implement the `getWeather()` method in the `WeatherServiceImpl` class. We use classes from the `Dom4j` and `Jaxen` libraries in this service. This also means that we need to add the two JAR files for these projects to the `buildpath` for our Eclipse project. `Dom4j` is a fast and easy-to-use XML parser, which supports searching XML via XPath expressions. The XPath support is itself provided by classes from the `Jaxen` project. We retrieve the response XML document by calling the Yahoo weather service URL with a ZIP code parameter. The returned XML is searched using XPath expressions. We add namespaces for `yweather` and `geo` to the XPath expression, as some of the elements in the response XML are under this different namespace:

```
document = reader.read(new URL
        ("http://xml.weather.yahoo.com/forecastrss?p=" + zipCode));
XPath expression = new Dom4jXPath("/rss/channel");
expression.addNamespace
```

```
("yweather","http://xml.weather.yahoo.com/ns/rss/1.0");
expression.addNamespace
("geo","http://www.w3.org/2003/01/geo/wgs84_pos#");
```

We then search the response using XPath, get the value we are interested in, and set the appropriate attribute for the weather object. So for instance, here is how we get the value for the city and state for this location, and set those properties for the weather object:

```
weather.setCity(result.valueOf("//yweather:location/@city"));
weather.setState(result.valueOf("//yweather:location/@region"));
```

We have to do something different for getting the image URL with the image for the current conditions. This URL is embedded in a CDATA section in the response. So we use an XPath expression to get the text for this node, and then access the substring that contains the IMG tag that we are looking for:

```
String descriptionSection = result.valueOf
                            ("/rss/channel/item/description");
weather.setImageUrl(descriptionSection.substring
                    (descriptionSection.indexOf("src=") + 5,
                    descriptionSection.indexOf(".gif") + 4));
```

The weather object with all these properties set is returned as the response from a call to this service. We now create our actual widget that will utilize and call this service. The user interface consists of a nice rounded panel that contains the following components:

- An image for the current conditions—the image URL.

- The actual text for the current condition—such as cloudy, sunny, etc.

- The current temperature.

- A section for displaying the current wind conditions—chill, direction, and speed.

- A section for displaying the current atmospheric conditions—humidity, visibility, and the barometric pressure and its direction of change.

- A section for displaying the current astronomical data—sunrise and sunset.

- A section for displaying the current geographic data—latitude and longitude for this location.

- A textbox for entering a new ZIP code.

The temperature is displayed in degrees, and the degrees symbol is shown by using the entity version — ° — in the code. So we display the current temperature in the widget like this:

```
tempPanel.add(new HTML("<div class='degrees'>&deg;</div>"));
```

The service is invoked asynchronously when this widget is initialized, and the corresponding display elements are set with their values when the response is received from the WeatherService. We recreate the JAR file, to contain this widget too, and then use this widget in the Samples project by instantiating it and adding it to a panel. Since we had already added the widgets.jar file to the classpath in the previous section, it should already be available to use in the Samples project. This sample is more complex than the calendar widget because it also includes an RPC service, in addition to the user interface. So when we use it, we need to add an entry for the service from this widget to the module XML file of the project, where the widget will be used:

```
<servlet path="/Samples/weather" class=
        "com.packtpub.gwtbook.widgets.server.WeatherServiceImpl"/>
```

Summary

In this chapter, we have learned about creating and reusing custom widgets. We created a calendar widget, where we could navigate forward and backward, and come back to the present date.

Then, we created a weather widget, which provided a weather information service for a particular place.

In the next chapter, we will learn how to create and run unit tests for testing GWT applications and RPC services.

8
Unit Tests

JUnit is a widely used open-source Java unit-testing framework created by Erich Gamma and Kent Beck (`http://junit.org`). It allows you to incrementally build a suite of tests as an integral part of your development effort and goes a long way towards increasing your confidence in the stability of your code base. JUnit was originally designed and used for testing Java classes, but has since been emulated and used in several other languages such as Ruby, Python, and C#. GWT utilizes and extends the JUnit framework to provide a way to test your AJAX code as simply as any other Java code. In this chapter, we will learn how to create and run unit tests for testing GWT applications and RPC services.

The tasks that we will address are:

- Test a GWT page
- Test an asynchronous service
- Test a GWT page with an asynchronous service
- Create and run a test suite

Test a GWT Page

A GWT page essentially consists of widgets and we can test the page by checking for the presence of the widgets and also by checking for the widget values or parameters that we want. In this section, we will learn how create a unit test for a GWT page.

Time for Action—Creating a Unit Test

We are going to test the `AutoFormFillPanel` page that we created in Chapter 4 by using the testing support built into the GWT framework to write our unit test.

The steps are as follows:

1. Run the GWT_HOME\junitCreator command script by providing these parameters:

    ```
    junitCreator -junit junit.jar -module com.packtpub.gwtbook.samples.
    Samples -eclipse Samples -out ~pchaganti/dev/GWTBook/Samples com.
    packtpub.gwtbook.samples.client.panels.AutoFormFillPanelTest
    ```

    ```
    pchaganti@pchaganti:~/dev/gwt-linux-1.1.10$ ./junitCreator -junit junit.jar -mod
    ule com.packtpub.gwtbook.samples.Samples -eclipse Samples -out ~pchaganti/GWTBoo
    k/Samples com.packtpub.gwtbook.samples.client.panels.AutoFormFillPanelTest
    Created directory /home/pchaganti/GWTBook/Samples/test
    Created directory /home/pchaganti/GWTBook/Samples/test/com/packtpub/gwtbook/samp
    les/client/panels
    Created file /home/pchaganti/GWTBook/Samples/test/com/packtpub/gwtbook/samples/c
    lient/panels/AutoFormFillPanelTest.java
    Created file /home/pchaganti/GWTBook/Samples/AutoFormFillPanelTest-hosted.launch
    Created file /home/pchaganti/GWTBook/Samples/AutoFormFillPanelTest-web.launch
    Created file /home/pchaganti/GWTBook/Samples/AutoFormFillPanelTest-hosted
    Created file /home/pchaganti/GWTBook/Samples/AutoFormFillPanelTest-web
    pchaganti@pchaganti:~/dev/gwt-linux-1.1.10$
    ```

2. Open the generated Java file com.packtpub.gwtbook.samples.client.
    panels.AutoFormFillPanelTest.java in the test directory that was
    automatically created when we ran the junitCreator command. Add a new
    method named testPanel() to the file:

    ```java
    public void testPanel()
    {
    }
    ```

3. Create the form and add assertions for checking the name of the Customer ID
    label and the style associated with it:

    ```java
    final AutoFormFillPanel autoFormFillPanel = new
      AutoFormFillPanel();
    assertEquals("Customer ID : ",
      autoFormFillPanel.getCustIDLbl().getText());
    assertEquals("autoFormItem-Label",
      autoFormFillPanel.getCustIDLbl().getStyleName());
    ```

4. Add similar assertions to test all the other elements on the page:

    ```java
    assertEquals("Address : ",
      autoFormFillPanel.getAddressLbl().getText());
    assertEquals("autoFormItem-Label",
      autoFormFillPanel.getAddressLbl().getStyleName());
    assertEquals("City : ",
      autoFormFillPanel.getCityLbl().getText());
    assertEquals("autoFormItem-Label",
    ```

```
        autoFormFillPanel.getCityLbl().getStyleName());
    assertEquals("First Name : ",
      autoFormFillPanel.getFirstNameLbl().getText());
    assertEquals("autoFormItem-Label",
      autoFormFillPanel.getFirstNameLbl().getStyleName());
    assertEquals("Last Name : ",
      autoFormFillPanel.getLastNameLbl().getText());
    assertEquals("autoFormItem-Label",
      autoFormFillPanel.getLastNameLbl().getStyleName());
    assertEquals("Phone Number : ",
      autoFormFillPanel.getPhoneLbl().getText());
    assertEquals("autoFormItem-Label",
      autoFormFillPanel.getPhoneLbl().getStyleName());
    assertEquals("State : ",
      autoFormFillPanel.getStateLbl().getText());
    assertEquals("autoFormItem-Label",
      autoFormFillPanel.getStateLbl().getStyleName());
    assertEquals("Zip Code : ",
      autoFormFillPanel.getZipLbl().getText());
    assertEquals("autoFormItem-Label",
      autoFormFillPanel.getZipLbl()
```

5. Add an entry to the `Samples.gwt.xml` file to inherit from the JUnit testing module:

```
<inherits name='com.google.gwt.junit.JUnit' />
```

6. Run the test in Eclipse by launching the `AutoFormFillPanelTest`-hosted launch configuration from the **Run** menu and get a similar screen to this:

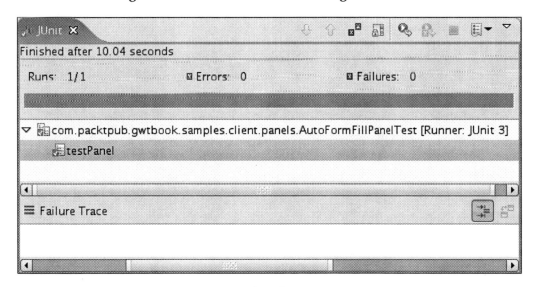

What Just Happened?

The GWT framework supports unit testing by providing the GWTTestCase base class that extends from TestCase in the JUnit testing library. We execute the unit tests by compiling and running the class that extends from GWTTestCase. An invisible web browser is launched by the GWT framework when we run this subclass, and the tests are run inside the browser instance.

We use the junitCreator command script provided by GWT to generate the scaffolding necessary for creating and running a unit test. We provide the name of the test class as one of the parameters to this command. A sample test case that extends from the GWTTestCase class is generated along with two launch scripts—one for running in the host mode and the other for running in the web mode. These launch configurations are generated in Eclipse format, and can be run directly from inside the Eclipse environment.

The class that extends GWTTestCase must implement getModuleMethod() and return the fully-qualified name of the GWT module that contains the test class. So in our case, we return com.packtpub.gwtbook.samples.Samples from this method. This enables GWT to resolve the dependencies and load the classes needed for running the test correctly. If we are creating tests in a completely separate module, this method will need to return the name of that containing module. We also need to inherit from the GWT JUnit module in the module file of our project. That is why we need to add this line to the Samples.gwt.xml file:

```
<inherits name='com.google.gwt.junit.JUnit' />
```

Using junitCreator is the simplest way to start using the unit testing features in GWT. However, if you decide to create the various artifacts that are generated by this command yourself, here are the steps involved in creating and running a unit test in your GWT project:

1. Create a class that extends GWTTestCase. Implement the getModuleName() method in this class to return the fully-qualified name of the module that contains this class.

2. Compile the test case. In order to run your test, you *must* compile it first.

3. In order to run the tests, your classpath must include junit-dev-linux.jar or gwt-dev-windows.jar file, and junit.jar file in addition to the normal requirements.

Since GWTTestCase is just a subclass of TestCase, you have access to all the normal assertion methods from the JUnit library. You can use these to assert and test all kinds of things about the page, such as the structure of the document, including tables and other HTML elements and their layout.

Test an Asynchronous Service

In the previous section, we learned how to create simple tests for unit testing a GWT page. However, most non-trivial GWT applications will access and use AJAX services to retrieve data asynchronously. In this section, we will go through the steps required to test an asynchronous service such as the `AutoFormFillPanel` service that we created earlier in this book.

Time for Action—Testing the Asynchronous Service

We are going to test `AutoFormFillPanelService`, which we created in Chapter 4:

1. Run the `GWT_HOME\junitCreator` command script by providing these parameters:

   ```
   junitCreator -junit junit.jar -module com.packtpub.gwtbook.samples.
   Samples -eclipse Samples -out ~pchaganti/dev/GWTBook/Samples com.
   packtpub.gwtbook.samples.client.panels.AutoFormFillServiceTest
   ```

2. Open the generated Java file `com.packtpub.gwtbook.samples.client.panels.AutoFormFillServiceTest.java` in the test directory that was automatically created when we ran the `junitCreator` command. Add a new method named `testService()` to the file:

   ```
   public void testService()
   {
   }
   ```

3. In the `testService()` method, instantiate `AutoFormFillService` and set the entry point information:

   ```
   final AutoFormFillServiceAsync autoFormFillService =
     (AutoFormFillServiceAsync) GWT.create
     (AutoFormFillService.class);
   ServiceDefTarget endpoint = (ServiceDefTarget)
     autoFormFillService;
   endpoint.setServiceEntryPoint("/Samples/autoformfill");
   ```

4. Create a new asynchronous callback, and in the `onSuccess()` method add assertions to test the data returned from invoking the service:

   ```
   AsyncCallback callback = new AsyncCallback()
   {
     public void onSuccess(Object result)
     {
       HashMap formValues = (HashMap) result;
   ```

```
      assertEquals("Joe", formValues.get("first name"));
      assertEquals("Customer", formValues.get("last name"));
      assertEquals("123 peachtree street",
        formValues.get("address"));
      assertEquals("Atlanta", formValues.get("city"));
      assertEquals("GA", formValues.get("state"));
      assertEquals("30339", formValues.get("zip"));
      assertEquals("770-123-4567", formValues.get("phone"));
      finishTest();
    }
  };
```

5. Call the `delayTestFinish()` method and invoke the asynchronous service:

    ```
    delayTestFinish(2000);
    autoFormFillService.getFormInfo("1111", callback);
    ```

6. Run the test in Eclipse by launching the `AutoFormFillPanelService`-hosted launch configuration from the **Run** menu. Here is the result:

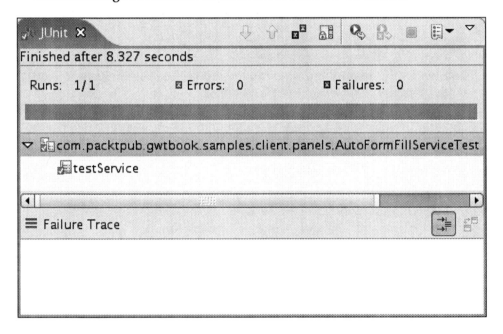

What Just Happened?

JUnit provides support for testing normal Java classes, but lacks any support for testing modules that have any kind of asynchronous behavior. A unit test will start executing and will run through all the tests in the module in order. This approach will not work for testing asynchronous things, where you make a request and the response comes back separately. GWT has this unique functionality, and supports tests for asynchronous services; so you can call an RPC service and validate the response from the service.

You can also test other long-running services, such as timers. In order to provide this support, `GWTTestCase` extends `TestCase` class and provides two methods— `delayTestFinish()` and `finishTest()` —which enable us to delay finishing a unit test, and have control over when the test actually completes. This essentially lets us put our unit test in an asynchronous mode, so we can wait for a response from a call to a remote server and complete the test by validating the response when we receive it.

In this sample, we structure our test using a standard pattern for testing long-lived events in GWT. The steps are as follows:

1. We create an instance of the asynchronous service and set its entry point.

2. We set up an asynchronous event handler, which is our callback. In this callback, we validate the received response by asserting the returned values match our expected values. We then complete the test by calling `finishTest()` to indicate to GWT that we want to leave the asynchronous mode in the test:

```
AsyncCallback callback = new AsyncCallback()
{
  public void onSuccess(Object result)
  {
    HashMap formValues = (HashMap) result;
    assertEquals("Joe", formValues.get("first name"));
    assertEquals("Customer", formValues.get("last name"));
    assertEquals("123 peachtree street",formValues.get
                                          ("address"));
    assertEquals("Atlanta", formValues.get("city"));
    assertEquals("GA", formValues.get("state"));
    assertEquals("30339", formValues.get("zip"));
    assertEquals("770-123-4567", formValues.get("phone"));
    finishTest();
  }
};
```

3. We set up a delay period for the test to finish. This makes the GWT test framework wait for the requisite amount of time. Here we set a delay of 2000 ms:

```
delayTestFinish(2000);
```

This must be set to a time period that is slightly longer than the time that the service is expected to take to return the response.

4. Finally, we invoke the asynchronous event, providing it the `callback` object as a parameter. In this case we just call the requisite method on `AutoFormFillService`:

```
autoFormFillService.getFormInfo("1111", callback);
```

You can use this pattern to test all asynchronous GWT services and classes that use timers.

Test a GWT Page with an Asynchronous Service

In this section, we will test a page that invokes an asynchronous service. This will enable us to create one test that combines the previous two examples.

Time for Action—Combining the Two

We are going to combine the two tests that we wrote in the last two sections into one, and create a comprehensive test for the `AutoFormFillPanel` page that tests both the page elements and the asynchronous service used by the page. The steps are as follows:

1. Add a new method named `simulateCustomerIDChanged()` to the existing `AutoFormFillPanel` class in the `com.packtpub.gwtbook.samples.client.panels` package:

```
public void simulateCustIDChanged(String custIDValue)
{
  if (custIDValue.length() > 0)
  {
    AsyncCallback callback = new AsyncCallback()
    {
      public void onSuccess(Object result)
      {
        setValues((HashMap) result);
      }
    };
    custID.setText(custIDValue);
    autoFormFillService.getFormInfo(custIDValue, callback);
  }
  else
  {
```

```
    clearValues();
  }
}
```

2. Modify the testPanel() method name to testEverything(). At the bottom
   of the method, invoke the simulateCustIDChanged() method and provide
   an ID parameter of 1111:

```
autoFormFillPanel.simulateCustIDChanged("1111");
```

3. Create a new Timer object, and add the following to its run() method:

```
Timer timer = new Timer()
{
  public void run()
  {
    assertEquals("Joe",
      autoFormFillPanel.getFirstName().getText());
    assertEquals("Customer",
      autoFormFillPanel.getLastName().getText());
    assertEquals("123 peachtree street",
      autoFormFillPanel.getAddress().getText());
    assertEquals("Atlanta",
      autoFormFillPanel.getCity().getText());
    assertEquals("GA", autoFormFillPanel.getState().getText());
    assertEquals("30339",
      autoFormFillPanel.getZip().getText());
    assertEquals("770-123-4567",
      autoFormFillPanel.getPhone().getText());
    finishTest();
  }
};
```

4. Delay the test finish and run the timer:

```
delayTestFinish(2000);
timer.schedule(100);
```

5. Run the test by launching the `AutoFormFillPanelTest`-hosted launch configuration and get a similar result to this:

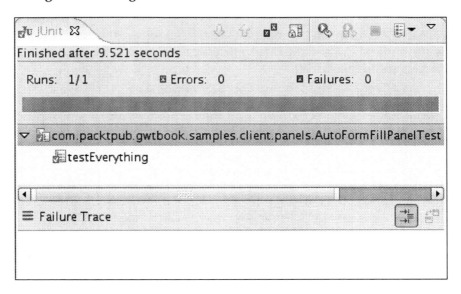

What Just Happened?

We have so far written two separate tests—one to test the various HTML elements on the `AutoFormFillPanel` page, and the other to test `AutoFormFillPanelService`. We can combine the two tests into one, and create a single test for testing the panel. `AutoFormFillPanel` invokes the asynchronous service when the text in the `CustomerID` textbox is changed. In order to simulate the keyboard listener in the test, we create a new public method called `simulateCustIDChanged()` in the `AutoFormFillPanel` class, which essentially does the same thing as the keyboard listener event handler in that class. We are going to call this method to simulate the text typed in by the user at the keyboard to change the `CustomerID` text.

Once we test the various HTML elements on the page, we invoke the `simulateCustIDChanged()` method. We then set up an asynchronous event handler using a `Timer` object. When the timer runs, we validate that the right values are available from the panel, as given in step 3.

We set up a delay for the test to finish:

```
delayTestFinish(2000);
```

Finally, we schedule the timer to run, so that when the timer fires after the given delay, it will validate the expected results and then complete the test:

```
timer.schedule(100);
```

Create and Run a Test Suite

We have so far learned how to create and run individual unit tests. As your code base increases, it is very tedious to run the tests all one at a time. JUnit provides the concept of a test suite that lets you combine a set of tests into one suite and run them. In this section, we are going to learn how to create and run multiple unit tests as part of a suite.

Time for Action—Deploying a Test Suite

We have so far been generating a test-launch script for every test that we create and running each test that we created separately. In this section, we will combine our tests into a test suite and run all of our tests in a single launch configuration. The steps are as follows:

1. Run the GWT_HOME\junitCreator command script by providing these parameters:

   ```
   junitCreator -junit junit.jar -module com.packtpub.gwtbook.samples.
   Samples -eclipse Samples -out ~pchaganti/dev/GWTBook/Samplescom.
   packtpub.gwtbook.samples.client.SamplesTestSuite
   ```

2. Modify the SamplesTestSuite class and add a suite() method:

   ```
   public static Test suite()
   {
     TestSuite samplesTestSuite = new TestSuite();
     samplesTestSuite.addTestSuite(AutoFormFillServiceTest.class);
     samplesTestSuite.addTestSuite(AutoFormFillPanelTest.class);
     return samplesTestSuite;
   }
   ```

3. Run the test by launching the `SamplesTestSuite`-hosted launch configuration and get a similar result to this:

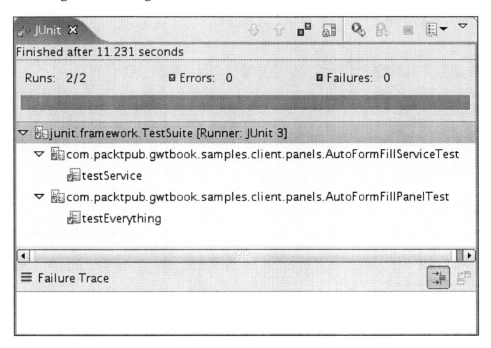

What Just Happened?

It can get tedious generating a separate launch script for each test that you write and then having to run each of these tests separately. Using a test suite lets us have one place to collect all of our tests. We can then use the launch script for the suite to run all the tests. A test suite is essentially a collector for all the tests in a project. We define a static factory method named `suite()` in our project. In this method, we add all the tests to the `suite` object, and return the `suite` object as the return value:

```
public static Test suite()
{
  TestSuite samplesTestSuite = new TestSuite();
  samplesTestSuite.addTestSuite(AutoFormFillServiceTest.class);
  samplesTestSuite.addTestSuite(AutoFormFillPanelTest.class);
  return samplesTestSuite;
}
```

When we run this test by launching the script, the JUnit framework recognizes that we are running a suite of tests, and it runs each of the tests defined in the suite. There is currently no support for inferring all the tests present in a GWT project and generating a test suite automatically to contain those tests. So you have to manually add each test that you want to be a part of the suite to this method. Now that we have the test suite working, we can delete all the other test launch configurations from our `Samples` project, and just use this one configuration for running all our tests.

Summary

In this chapter, we have learned to create unit test for a GWT page (`AutoFormFillPanel`) and an asynchronous service (`AutoFormFillPanelService`). We then combined these two and created a unit test for a GWT page that uses an asynchronous service.

Finally, we combined all our tests into a test suite and ran all of our tests in a single launch configuration.

In the next chapter, we will learn about the internationalization (I18N) and XML support in GWT.

9

I18N and XML

In this chapter, we will learn how to use internationalization in a GWT application. We will also create samples that showcase GWT support for the client-side creation and parsing of XML documents.

The tasks that we will address are:

- Internationalization
- Create XML documents
- Parse XML documents

Internationalization (I18N)

GWT provides extensive support for creating applications that can display text in a wide variety of languages. In this section, we are going to utilize GWT to create a page that can display text in the appropriate language for a given locale.

Time for Action—Using the I18N Support

We are going to create a simple GWT user interface that displays the appropriate image and translation for the text "Welcome" for the specified locale. The image displayed will be the flag that corresponds to the chosen locale. The steps are as follows:

1. Create a new Java file named I18NSamplesConstants.java in the com. packtpub.gwtbook.samples.client.util package that defines an interface named I18NSamplesConstants. Add the following two methods to the interface—one for retrieving the welcome text and one for retrieving the image:

```
public interface I18NSamplesConstants extends Constants
{
  String welcome();
```

```
        String flag_image();
}
```

2. Create a new file named `I18NSamplesConstants.properties` in the `com.packtpub.gwtbook.samples.client.util` package. Add the properties for the welcome text and the image to it:

```
welcome = Welcome
flag_image = flag_en.gif
```

This properties file represents the default locale, in this case US English.

3. Create a new file named `I18NSamplesConstants_el_GR.properties` in the `com.packtpub.gwtbook.samples.client.util` package. Add the properties for the welcome text and the image to it:

```
welcome = υποδοχή
flag_image = flag_el_GR.gif
```

This properties file represents the locale for Greek.

4. Create a new file named `I18NSamplesConstants_es_ES.properties` in the `com.packtpub.gwtbook.samples.client.util` package. Add the properties for the welcome text and the image to it:

```
welcome = recepción
flag_image = flag_es_ES.gif
```

This properties file represents the locale for Spanish.

5. Create a new file named `I18NSamplesConstants_zh_CN.properties` in the `com.packtpub.gwtbook.samples.client.util` package. Add the properties for the welcome text and the image to it:

```
welcome = 歡迎
flag_image = flag_zh_CN.gif
```

This properties file represents the locale for Chinese.

6. Create a new Java file named `I18NPanel.java` in the `com.packtpub.gwtbook.samples.client.panels` package. Create `VerticalPanel` that will contain the user interface. We will add this panel into `DockPanel` and add it into our `Samples` application, like all the other applications that we have been working on in this book. Add a label that will display the welcome text message in the appropriate language for the provided locale:

```
private VerticalPanel workPanel = new VerticalPanel();
private Label welcome = new Label();
```

7. Create an instance of I18NSamplesConstants in the constructor. Add an image widget for displaying the flag image and a label for displaying the welcome text to the panel. Set the text for the label and the image file by using I18NSamplesConstants. Finally, create a little info panel that displays descriptive text about this application, so that we can display the text when this sample is selected in the list of available samples in our Samples application. Add the info panel and the work panel to a dock panel, and initialize the widget:

```
public I18nPanel()
{
  I18NSamplesConstants myConstants = (I18NSamplesConstants)
    GWT.create(I18NSamplesConstants.class);
  // Always the same problem, samples are not "sound
    and complete"
  welcome.setText(myConstants.welcome());
  welcome.setStyleName("flagLabel");
  Image flag = new Image("images/" + myConstants.flag_image());
  flag.setStyleName("flag");
  workPanel.add(flag);
  workPanel.add(welcome);
  DockPanel workPane = new DockPanel();
  workPane.add(infoPanel, DockPanel.NORTH);
  workPane.add(workPanel, DockPanel.CENTER);
  workPane.setCellHeight(workPanel, "100%");
  workPane.setCellWidth(workPanel, "100%");
  initWidget(workPane);
}
```

8. Add an entry to import the I18N module to the Samples.gwt.xml file:

```
<inherits name ="com.google.gwt.i18n.I18N"/>
```

9. Add an entry for each locale that we support to the Samples.gwt.xml file:

```
<extend-property name="locale" values-"el_GR"/>
<extend-property name="locale" values="es_ES"/>
<extend-property name="locale" values="zh_CN"/>
```

Run the application. Here is the default interface displayed in the default locale—`en_US`:

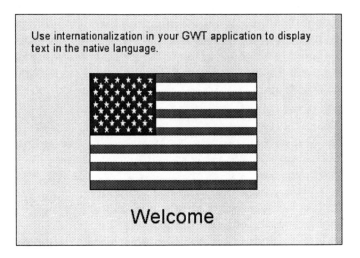

Modify the URL to add a locale query parameter with each of the locales that we support to see the user interface displayed in the appropriate language. Here is the user interface displayed in Greek—`el_GR`:

```
http://localhost:8888/com.packtpub.gwtbook.samples.Samples/
Samples.html?locale=el_GR#i18n
```

Here is the user interface displayed in Spanish—`es_ES`:

```
http://localhost:8888/com.packtpub.gwtbook.samples.Samples/
Samples.html?locale=es_ES#i18n
```

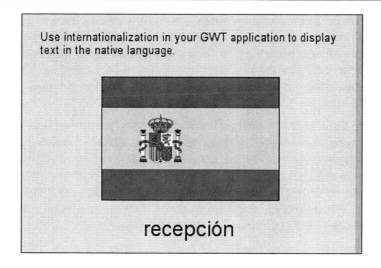

Here is the user interface displayed in Chinese — zh_CN:

```
http://localhost:8888/com.packtpub.gwtbook.samples.Samples/
Samples.html?locale=zh_CN#i18n
```

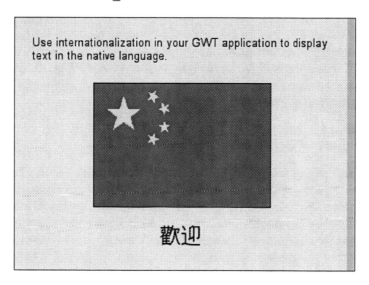

What Just Happened?

GWT provides various tools and techniques that help in developing
internationalized applications that can display text in various languages. There are
two main techniques for developing internationalized applications using GWT:

- **Static String Internationalization**: This is a type-safe technique that depends on Java interfaces and regular properties files. It generates code from the previous two components to provide an application with messages that are aware of the locale whose context they are operating in. This technique is recommended for new applications that do not have existing localized properties files.

- **Dynamic String Internationalization**: This technique is used when you already have an existing localization system, such as your web server that can generate localized strings. These translated strings are then printed within your HTML page. This approach is usually slower than the static approach, but since it does not have the code generation phase, you do not need to recompile your application every time your message strings are modified, or the list of locales supported is changed.

In this sample, we are using the static internationalization technique. We create an interface I18NSamplesConstants that defines two methods — one method returns the welcome message, while the other method returns the flag-image file name. We then create a properties file for each locale supported by our application, and add the messages in the appropriate language to the file.

A locale is an object that uniquely identifies a particular combination of language and a region. So for instance, a locale of en_US refers to the language as English and the region as United States. Similarly, fr_FR refers to the language French and the region France. The properties file name must end with the locale identifier before the extension properties. Here are the contents of our properties file for Spanish language in the region Spain:

```
welcome = recepción
flag_image = flag_es_ES.gif
```

Our user interface is very simple, and it consists of one image with a label under it. The image will display the flag of the region whose locale we are using, and the label will display the welcome text in the language for the locale. The application on startup will display the page in the default locale for your environment. You can change this by appending a query parameter with the key locale and a value equal to any of the supported locales. So in order to view the page in Greek, you would append locale=el_GR to the respective URL.

If you provide a locale that is not supported, the web page will be displayed
in the default locale. We access the appropriate text by creating the
I18NSamplesConstants class, using the accessors to get the localized messages, and
setting the values for the two widgets:

```
I18NSamplesConstants myConstants = (I18NSamplesConstants)
GWT.create(I18NSamplesConstants.class);
welcome.setText(myConstants.welcome());
Image flag = new Image("images/" + myConstants.flag_image());
```

The I18NSamplesConstants class extends from the Constants class, which enables
binding at compile time to constant values that are acquired from simple property
files. When we use GWT.create() method to instantiate I18NSamplesConstants,
GWT automatically generates the right subclass that uses values from the property
file for the appropriate locale and returns it. The supported locales themselves are
defined by the module file, using an extend-property tag. This informs the GWT
framework that we want to extend the default property "locale", by providing
alternatives for it:

```
<extend-property name="locale" values="el_GR"/>
```

We also inherit from com.google.gwt.i18n.I18N in the Samples.gwt.xml file so
that our module can have access to the I18N functionality provided by GWT.

There are several other tools provided by GWT to enhance the I18N support.
There is a Messages class that can be used when we want to provide localized
messages that have parameters passed to them. We can also ignore the localization,
and use a regular properties file to store configuration information. We also have
an i18nCreator command script that can generate the Constants or Messages
interfaces and sample properties files. Finally, a Dictionary class is also available
that can be used for dynamic internationalization, as it provides a way to dynamically
look up key-value pairs of strings that are defined in the HTML page for the module.

The I18N support in GWT is quite extensive and can be used to support either simple
or complicated internationalization scenarios.

Creating XML Documents

XML is in wide-spread use across enterprises in a variety of applications, and is also
very commonly used when integrating disparate systems. In this section, we will
learn about GWT's XML support and how to use it to create an XML document on
the client side.

Time for Action—Creating an XML Document

We are going to take customer data stored in a CSV file, and create an XML document containing the customer data. The steps are as follows:

1. Create a simple CSV file with the customer data in a file named `customers.csv` in the `com.packtpub.gwtbook.samples.public` package. Add the information for two customers to this file:

    ```
    John Doe,222 Peachtree St,Atlanta
    Jane Doe,111 10th St,New York
    ```

2. Create the user interface in a new Java file named `CreateXMLPanel.java` in the package `com.packtpub.gwtbook.samples.client.panels`. Create a private `HTMLPanel` variable that will display the XML document that we are going to create. Also create a `VerticalPanel` class that will be the container for the user interface:

    ```
    private HTMLPanel htmlPanel = new HTMLPanel("<pre></pre>");
    private VerticalPanel workPanel = new VerticalPanel();
    ```

3. Create a private method named `createXMLDocument()` that can take a string and create the customer's XML document from it. Create an XML document object, add the processing instruction for the XML version, and create a root node named `customers`. Loop through the customer information on each row from the CSV file. Create the appropriate XML nodes, set their value, and add them to the root node. Finally return the XML document created:

    ```
    private Document createXMLDocument(String data)
    {
      String[] tokens = data.split("\n");
      Document customersDoc = XMLParser.createDocument();
      ProcessingInstruction procInstruction = customersDoc.
      createProcessingInstruction("xml", "version=\"1.0\"");
      customersDoc.appendChild(procInstruction);
      Element rootElement =
        customersDoc.createElement("customers");
      customersDoc.appendChild(rootElement);
      for (int i = 0; i < tokens.length; i++)
      {
        String[] customerInfo = tokens[i].split(",");
        Element customerElement =
          customersDoc.createElement("customer");
        Element customerNameElement =
          customersDoc.createElement("name");
        customerNameElement.appendChild
          (customersDoc.createTextNode(customerInfo[0]));
    ```

```
   Element customerAddressElement =
     customersDoc.createElement("address");
   customerAddressElement.appendChild
     (customersDoc.createTextNode(customerInfo[1]));
   Element customerCityElement =
     customersDoc.createElement("city");
   customerCityElement.appendChild
     (customersDoc.createTextNode(customerInfo[2]));
   customerElement.appendChild(customerNameElement);
   customerElement.appendChild(customerAddressElement);
   customerElement.appendChild(customerCityElement);
   rootElement.appendChild(customerElement);
 }
 return customersDoc;
}
```

4. Create a new method named `createPrettyXML()` that will format our XML document nicely by indenting the nodes before we display it in `HTMLPanel`:

```
private String createPrettyXML(Document xmlDoc)
{
String xmlString = xmlDoc.toString();
xmlString = xmlString.replaceAll
  ("<customers", "  <customers");
xmlString = xmlString.replaceAll
  ("</customers","  </customers");
xmlString = xmlString.replaceAll
  ("<customer>","   <customer>");
xmlString = xmlString.replaceAll
  ("</customer>","   </customer>");
xmlString = xmlString.replaceAll("<name>",
  "    <name>  
     ");
xmlString = xmlString.replaceAll("</name>",
  "\n    </name>");
xmlString = xmlString.replaceAll("<address>",
  "    <address>  
     ");
xmlString = xmlString.replaceAll("</address>",
  "\n    </address>");
xmlString = xmlString.replaceAll("<city>",
  "    <city>  
     ");
xmlString = xmlString.replaceAll("</city>",
  "\n    </city>");
```

```
      xmlString = xmlString.replaceAll(">", ">\n");
      xmlString = xmlString.replaceAll("<", "&#60;");
      xmlString = xmlString.replaceAll(">", "&#62;");
      return xmlString;
    }
```

This is just a quick-and-dirty way of formatting the XML document, as GWT does not currently provide a nice way to do this.

5. Create the user interface for this application in a new Java file named `CreateXMLPanel.java` in the `com.packtpub.gwtbook.samples.client.panels` package. In the constructor `CreateXMLPanel()`, make an asynchronous HTTP request to get the `customers.csv` file. On success, create the XML document from the data contained in the CSV file and display it in the `HTMLPanel`. Finally, create a little info panel that displays descriptive text about this application, so that we can display the text when this sample is selected in the list of available samples in our `Samples` application. Add the info panel and the work panel to a dock panel, and initialize the widget:

```
public CreateXMLPanel()
{
  HorizontalPanel infoPanel = new HorizontalPanel();
  infoPanel.add(new HTML(
    "<div class='infoProse'>Read a comma separated text file
      and create an XML document from it.</div>"));
  HTTPRequest.asyncGet("customers.csv",
    new ResponseTextHandler()
    {
      public void onCompletion(String responseText)
      {
        Document customersDoc = createXMLDocument(responseText);
        if (htmlPanel.isAttached())
        {
          workPanel.remove(htmlPanel);
        }
        htmlPanel = new HTMLPanel("<pre>" +
        createPrettyXML(customersDoc) + "</pre>");
        htmlPanel.setStyleName("xmlLabel");
        workPanel.add(htmlPanel);
      }
    });
  DockPanel workPane = new DockPanel();
  workPane.add(infoPanel, DockPanel.NORTH);
  workPane.add(workPanel, DockPanel.CENTER);
```

```
            workPane.setCellHeight(workPanel, "100%");
            workPane.setCellWidth(workPanel, "100%");
            initWidget(workPane);
        }
```

6. Add an entry to import the XML module to the `Samples.gwt.xml` file:

```
<inherits name ="com.google.gwt.xml.XML"/>
```

Here is the page displaying the XML document created from the customer's CSV file:

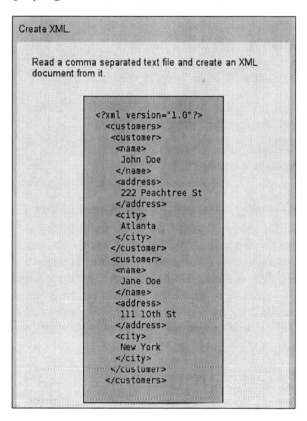

What Just Happened?

GWT provides good support for generating XML documents on the client side, and like everything else in the framework, it is browser-independent. You can utilize the `XMLParser` class to generate the documents, and can be assured that the XML document will be generated correctly in all the supported browsers. In this example, we create a simple CSV file with the customer data. This customer data is retrieved by using the `asyncGet()` method on the `HTTPRequest` object. Since there is no support provided for reading files from the file system in GWT, this is a workaround to load external files without resorting to using RPC services. We provide the name of the file and `ResponseTextHandler` as parameters to this method. `ResponseTextHandler` provides a callback that is executed when the synchronous call is completed. In the callback, we read in the contents of the response and create an XML document with the values. A new document is created by using the `XMLParser` object:

```
Document customersDoc = XMLParser.createDocument();
```

A processing instruction is added first to this document, so that the XML is well formed:

```
ProcessingInstruction procInstruction =
    customersDoc.createProcessingInstruction("XML", "version=\"1.0\"");
customersDoc.appendChild(procInstruction);
```

We then create the root node and child node. We add a text node to the new node with the value that we have parsed from the CSV file:

```
customersDoc.createElement("name");
customerNameElement.appendChild
                        (customersDoc.createTextNode(customerInfo[0]));
```

This new document is displayed by using a pre-formatted block in `HTMLPanel`. However, we need to format and indent the text nicely before displaying it in the panel; otherwise the entire document will appear as one line string. We have a private method that indents and formats the document nicely by using regular expressions. This is slightly tedious. Hopefully, in the future GWT will support creating pretty XML document in the framework itself. In this example, we are retrieving the contents of the CSV file via an HTTP request; we can provide the data for generating the XML in any format we like by using an RPC service.

Parse XML Documents

In the previous section, we used the GWT support for creating XML documents. In this section, we are going to learn how to read XML documents. We will be creating an application that can parse an XML file and populate a table using the data from the file.

Time for Action—Parsing XML on the Client

We will be creating a GWT application that can read an XML file containing information about some books, and populate a table with that data. The steps are as follows:

1. Create a simple XML file with the books' data in a file named `books.xml` in the `com.packtpub.gwtbook.samples.client.public` package:

    ```xml
    <?xml version="1.0" encoding="US-ASCII"?>
    <books>
      <book id="1">
        <title>I Claudius</title>
        <author>Robert Graves</author>
        <year>1952</year>
        </book>
      <book id="2">
        <title>The Woman in white</title>
        <author>Wilkie Collins</author>
        <year>1952</year>
      </book>
      <book id="3">
        <title>Shogun</title>
        <author>James Clavell</author>
        <year>1952</year>
      </book>
      <book id="4">
        <title>City of Djinns</title>
        <author>William Dalrymple</author>
        <year>2003</year>
      </book>
      <book id="5">
        <title>Train to pakistan</title>
        <author>Kushwant Singh</author>
        <year>1952</year>
      </book>
    </books>
    ```

2. Create the user interface for this application in a new Java file named `ParseXMLPanel.java` in the `com.packtpub.gwtbook.samples.client.panels` package. Create a `VerticalPanel` class that will contain our user interface, and a `FlexTable` class that we will use for displaying the data from the XML file:

    ```java
    private VerticalPanel workPanel = new VerticalPanel();
    private FlexTable booksTable = new FlexTable();
    ```

3. Create a private method named `getElementTextValue()` that can take a parent XML element and a tag name, and return the text value for that node:

```
private String getElementTextValue
  (Element parent, String elementTag)
{
  return parent.getElementsByTagName
    (elementTag).item(0).getFirstChild().getNodeValue();
}
```

4. In the constructor `ParseXMLPanel()`, add the table headers and styles for the flex table:

```
booksTable.setWidth(500 + "px");
booksTable.setStyleName("xmlParse-Table");
booksTable.setBorderWidth(1);
booksTable.setCellPadding(4);
booksTable.setCellSpacing(1);
booksTable.setText(0, 0, "Title");
booksTable.setText(0, 1, "Author");
booksTable.setText(0, 2, "Publication Year");
RowFormatter rowFormatter = booksTable.getRowFormatter();
rowFormatter.setStyleName(0, "xmlParse-TableHeader");
```

5. In the same constructor, make an asynchronous HTTP request to get the `books.xml` file, and on completion, parse the XML document and populate a flex table with the data. Finally, create a little info panel that displays descriptive text about this application, so that we can display the text when this sample is selected in the list of available samples in our `Samples` application. Add the info panel and the work panel to a dock panel, and initialize the widget:

```
HTTPRequest.asyncGet("books.xml", new ResponseTextHandler()
{
  public void onCompletion(String responseText)
  {
    Document bookDom = XMLParser.parse(responseText);
    Element booksElement = bookDom.getDocumentElement();
    XMLParser.removeWhitespace(booksElement);
    NodeList bookElements =
      booksElement.getElementsByTagName("book");
    for (int i = 0; i < bookElements.getLength(); i++)
    {
      Element bookElement = (Element) bookElements.item(i);
      booksTable.setText(i + 1, 0, getElementTextValue(
        bookElement, "title"));
```

```
            booksTable.setText(i + 1, 1, getElementTextValue(
                bookElement, "author"));
            booksTable.setText(i + 1, 2, getElementTextValue(
                bookElement, "year"));
        }
    }
});
DockPanel workPane = new DockPanel();
workPanel.add(booksTable);
workPane.add(infoPanel, DockPanel.NORTH);
workPane.add(workPanel, DockPanel.CENTER);
workPane.setCellHeight(workPanel, "100%");
workPane.setCellWidth(workPanel, "100%");
initWidget(workPane);
```

Here is the page with the table containing the data from the books.xml file:

Parse XML and populate a table with that data.

Title	Author	Publication Year
I,Claudius	Robert Graves	1934
The Woman in white	Wilkie Collins	1859
Shogun	James Clavell	1975
City of Djinns	William Dalrymple	1994
Train to pakistan	Kushwant Singh	1956

What Just Happened?

We once again use the HTTPRequest object to retrieve the contents of a file on the server, in this case the books.xml file, which contains some data on published books that we want to display in a table on the page. The XMLParser object is utilized to read in the contents of the asynchronous response into a document. This XML document is then traversed using the familiar DOM API, and the text values of the appropriate nodes are retrieved and used to populate the respective column cells in the flex table. We use the getElementsByTagName() method to get a NodeList that contains all the book elements:

```
NodeList bookElements = booksElement.getElementsByTagName("book");
```

Once we have this list, we just iterate through its child nodes, and access the values we are interested in:

```
for (int i = 0; i < bookElements.getLength(); i++)
{
  Element bookElement = (Element) bookElements.item(i);
  booksTable.setText(i + 1, 0, getElementTextValue(
                                       bookElement, "title"));
  booksTable.setText(i + 1, 1, getElementTextValue(
                                       bookElement, "author"));
  booksTable.setText(i + 1, 2, getElementTextValue(
                                       bookElement, "year"));
}
```

We inherit from the `com.google.gwt.xml.xml` file in the `Samples.gwt.xml` file so that our module can have access to the XML functionality provided by GWT.

Summary

In this chapter, we learned how to create an application with internationalization (I18N) support. We created a page that can display text in the appropriate language for a given locale. Then, we created an XML document on the client side using GWT's XML support.

Finally, we created an application that can parse an XML file and populate a table using the data from the file.

In the next chapter, we will learn how to deploy our GWT application in Tomcat.

10
Deployment

In this chapter, we will first learn how to manually deploy GWT applications, so we can gain familiarity with all the artifacts that are part of the deployment. We will then automate this process by using Apache Ant.

The tasks that we will address are:

- Manual deployment in Tomcat
- Automated deployment using Ant
- Deployment from Eclipse

Manual Deployment in Tomcat

We are going to take the `Samples` application that we have been working on in this book, and go through the various steps needed to have it manually deployed and running in Tomcat.

Time for Action—Deploying a GWT Application

Here are the steps required to manually deploy a GWT application to Tomcat:

1. Download and install Apache Tomcat for your platform (`http://tomcat.apache.org`). Select the latest stable version from the 5.x series. I am going to refer to the directory where Tomcat is installed as `$TOMCAT_DIR`, and the directory that contains the `Samples` project as `$SAMPLES_DIR`.

2. Run `$SAMPLES_DIR/Samples-compile` to compile the entire application. This will create a new directory named `www` under `$SAMPLES_DIR`.

3. Create a new file named `web.xml` in the `$SAMPLES_DIR` directory. Add a display name and a description for our application:

```
<display-name>
 GWT Book Samples
</display-name>
<description>
  GWT Book Samples
</description>
```

The display name is displayed when you browse the list of deployed applications using the Tomcat manager.

4. In the `web.xml` file created in the previous step, add entries for each of the RPC services we are using in our application and a corresponding servlet mapping for each entry. Add an entry for the live-search service:

```
<servlet>
  <servlet-name>livesearch</servlet-name>
  <servlet-class>
    com.packtpub.gwtbook.samples.server.
      LiveSearchServiceImpl
  </servlet-class>
</servlet>
<servlet-mapping>
  <servlet-name>livesearch</servlet-name>
  <url-pattern>/livesearch</url-pattern>
</servlet-mapping>
```

5. Add an entry for the password-strength service:

```
<servlet>
  <servlet-name>pwstrength</servlet-name>
  <servlet-class>
    com.packtpub.gwtbook.samples.server.
      PasswordStrengthServiceImpl
  </servlet-class>
</servlet>
<servlet-mapping>
  <servlet-name>pwstrength</servlet-name>
  <url-pattern>/pwstrength</url-pattern>
</servlet-mapping>
```

6. Add an entry for the auto-form-fill service:

```
<servlet>
  <servlet-name>autoformfill</servlet-name>
  <servlet-class>
    com.packtpub.gwtbook.samples.server.
```

```
    AutoFormFillServiceImpl
  </servlet-class>
</servlet>
<servlet-mapping>
  <servlet-name>autoformfill</servlet-name>
  <url-pattern>/autoformfill</url-pattern>
</servlet-mapping>
```

7. Add an entry for the dynamic-lists service:

```
<servlet>
  <servlet-name>dynamiclists</servlet-name>
  <servlet-class>
    com.packtpub.gwtbook.samples.server.
      DynamicListsServiceImpl
  </servlet-class>
</servlet>
<servlet-mapping>
  <servlet-name>dynamiclists</servlet-name>
  <url-pattern>/dynamiclists</url-pattern>
</servlet-mapping>
```

8. Add an entry for the pageable-data service:

```
<servlet>
  <servlet-name>pageabledata</servlet-name>
  <servlet-class>
    com.packtpub.gwtbook.samples.server.
      PageableDataServiceImpl
  </servlet-class>
</servlet>
<servlet-mapping>
  <servlet-name>pageabledata</servlet-name>
  <url-pattern>/pageabledata</url-pattern>
</servlet-mapping>
```

9. Add an entry for the live-data-grid service:

```
<servlet>
  <servlet-name>livedatagrid</servlet-name>
  <servlet-class>
    com.packtpub.gwtbook.samples.server.
      LiveDatagridServiceImpl
  </servlet-class>
</servlet>
<servlet-mapping>
  <servlet-name>livedatagrid</servlet-name>
```

```
    <url-pattern>/livedatagrid</url-pattern>
  </servlet-mapping>
```

10. Add an entry for the log-spy service:

```
<servlet>
  <servlet-name>logspy</servlet-name>
  <servlet-class>
    com.packtpub.gwtbook.samples.server.
      LogSpyServiceImpl
  </servlet-class>
</servlet>
<servlet-mapping>
  <servlet-name>logspy</servlet-name>
  <url-pattern>/logspy</url-pattern>
</servlet-mapping>
```

11. Add an entry for the weather service:

```
<servlet>
  <servlet-name>weather</servlet-name>
  <servlet-class>
    com.packtpub.gwtbook.widgets.server.
      WeatherServiceImpl
  </servlet-class>
</servlet>
<servlet-mapping>
  <servlet-name>weather</servlet-name>
  <url-pattern>/weather</url-pattern>
</servlet-mapping>
```

12. Add an entry for the welcome file and set the welcome file to the main HTML page for our application—`Samples.html`:

```
<welcome-file-list>
  <welcome-file>
    Samples.html
  </welcome-file>
</welcome-file-list>
```

13. Create a new directory named `WEB-INF` under the `www/com.packtpub.gwtbook.samples.Samples` directory. Create two subdirectories `lib` and `classes` under the `WEB-INF` directory.

14. Copy the above `web.xml` file to the `WEB-INF` directory.

15. Copy the contents of `$SAMPLES_DIR/bin` to the `WEB-INF/classes` directory.

16. Copy the contents of `$SAMPLES_DIR/lib` to the `WEB-INF/lib` directory.

17. Copy the `www/com.packtpub.gwtbook.samples.Samples` directory to `$TOMCAT_DIR/webapps`.

18. Start up Tomcat. Once it is up and running, navigate to the following URL to see the `Samples` application that we have created in this book:

    `http://localhost:8080/com.packtpub.gwtbook.samples.Samples/`

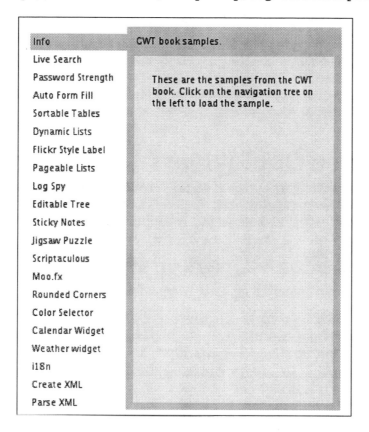

What Just Happened?

Compiling a GWT application generates HTML and JavaScript for the application in the www directory. This contains all the artifacts needed for the user interface and can actually be run on any web server. However, if you are using any RPC services, then you need to ensure that any third-party JARs needed by the services along with the service and support classes are deployed to a servlet container along with the contents of the www directory. We have chosen Tomcat for this, as it is one of the most widely used servlet containers and is the reference implementation for the JSP and Servlet specifications. We can similarly deploy our application to any other container such as Geronimo, JBoss, WebSphere, JOnAS, or Weblogic.

Deploying to a servlet container such as Tomcat implies that we structure our deployment to mimic the WAR format. So we need to ensure that all the Java classes from our application are available in the `WEB-INF/classes` directory, and all the JAR files used by our application need to be in the `WEB-INF/lib` directory. Accordingly, we copy those artifacts to these directories. We also create a deployment descriptor that is needed for Tomcat to recognize our deployment. This file is `web.xml`, and it needs to be copied to the `WEB-INF` directory.

Once we have everything in place in the `www/com.packtpub.gwtbook.samples.Samples` directory, we copy `com.packtpub.gwtbook.samples.Samples` to the web applications directory for Tomcat—`$TOMCAT_DIR/webapps`. Then we start Tomcat, which on startup will register the application from the `web.xml` file and make it available at the context—`com.packtpub.gwtbook.samples.Samples`.

Automated Deployment Using Ant

We are going to make things easier on ourselves and reduce the tedious work, by letting Ant handle the deployment of our GWT application. We will automate everything we did in the previous section by using Apache Ant.

Time for Action—Creating the Ant Build File

Here are the steps for automating the deployment to Tomcat:

1. We will modify the `$SAMPLES_DIR/Samples.ant.xml` file that was created when we ran `applicationCreator` to create our project in Chapter 3. Create global properties to refer various directories:

    ```
    <property name="tmp" value="${basedir}/build" />
    <property name="www" value=
      "${basedir}/www/com.packtpub.gwtbook.samples.Samples" />
    <property name="lib" value="${basedir}/lib" />
    <property name="classes" value="${basedir}/bin" />
    <property name="gwt-home" value="/gwt-windows-1.3.1" />
    <property name="deploy-dir" value=
      " /shonu/jakarta-tomcat-5.0.28/webapps" />
    ```

2. Add the JARs that we will need while compiling to the `classpath`:

    ```
    <pathelement path="${lib}/junit.jar"/>
    <pathelement path="${lib}/widgets.jar"/>
    <pathelement path="${lib}/gwt-widgets-0.1.3.jar"/>
    ```

3. Modify the `clean` target to include other artifacts to clean up:

    ```
    <target name="clean" description=
      "Clean up the build artifacts">
      <delete file="Samples.jar"/>
    ```

```
     <delete file="Samples.war"/>
     <delete>
       <fileset dir="bin" includes="**/*.class"/>
       <fileset dir="build" includes="**/*"/>
       <fileset dir="www" includes="**/*"/>
     </delete>
   </target>
```

4. Create a new target named `create-war`:

```
   <target name="create-war" depends="package" description=
     "Create a war file">
   <mkdir dir="${tmp}"/>
   <exec executable="${basedir}/Samples-compile.cmd"
     output="build-log.txt"/>
   <copy todir="${tmp}">
     <fileset dir="${www}" includes="**/*.*"/>
   </copy>
   <mkdir dir="${tmp}/WEB-INF" />
   <copy todir="${tmp}/WEB-INF">
     <fileset dir="${basedir}" includes="web.xml"/>
   </copy>
   <mkdir dir="${tmp}/WEB-INF/classes" />
   <copy todir="${tmp}/WEB-INF/classes">
     <fileset dir="${basedir}/bin" includes="**/*.*"/>
   </copy>
   <mkdir dir="${tmp}/WEB-INF/lib" />
   <copy todir="${tmp}/WEB-INF/lib">
     <fileset dir="${basedir}/lib" includes="**/*.jar" excludes=
        "gwt-dev-*.jar,gwt-servlet.jar,gwt-user.jar,*.so"/>
   </copy>
   <jar destfile="${tmp}/WEB-INF/lib/gwt-user-deploy.jar">
     <zipfileset src="${gwt-home}/gwt-user.jar">
       <exclude name="javax/**"/>
       <exclude name="META-INF/**"/>
       <exclude name="**/*.java"/>
     </zipfileset>
   </jar>
   <zip destfile="Samples.war"  basedir="${tmp}" />
   </target>
```

5. Create a new target named `deploy-war`:

```
   <target name="deploy-war" depends="clean,create-war"
     description="Deploy the war file">
   <copy todir="${deploy-dir}">
       <fileset dir="${basedir}" includes="Samples.war"/>
   </copy>
   </target>
```

6. Install Apache Ant if you do not already have it (http://ant.apache.org). Make sure that the Ant binary is on your path.

7. Run Ant from $SAMPLES_DIR with these parameters:

```
ant -f Samples.ant.xml deploy-war
```

This will clean the build artifacts, compile the entire application, create a WAR file, and deploy the WAR file to Tomcat. You can access the deployed application at the URL http://localhost:8080/Samples.

Here is the output when you run Ant:

```
pchaganti@pchaganti:~/dev/gwt-examples/GWTBook/Samples$ ant -f Samples.ant.xml deploy-war
Buildfile: Samples.ant.xml

clean:
    [delete] Deleting: /home/pchaganti/dev/gwt-examples/GWTBook/Samples/Samples.jar
    [delete] Deleting: /home/pchaganti/dev/gwt-examples/GWTBook/Samples/Samples.war
    [delete] Deleting 140 files from /home/pchaganti/dev/gwt-examples/GWTBook/Samples/bin
    [delete] Deleting 293 files from /home/pchaganti/dev/gwt-examples/GWTBook/Samples/build
    [delete] Deleting 89 files from /home/pchaganti/dev/gwt-examples/GWTBook/Samples/www

compile:
    [javac] Compiling 56 source files to /home/pchaganti/dev/gwt-examples/GWTBook/Samples/bin
    [javac] Note: Some input files use or override a deprecated API.
    [javac] Note: Recompile with -Xlint:deprecation for details.

package:
    [jar] Building jar: /home/pchaganti/dev/gwt-examples/GWTBook/Samples/Samples.jar

create-war:
    [copy] Copying 89 files to /home/pchaganti/dev/gwt-examples/GWTBook/Samples/build
    [copy] Copying 1 file to /home/pchaganti/dev/gwt-examples/GWTBook/Samples/build/WEB-INF
    [copy] Copying 186 files to /home/pchaganti/dev/gwt-examples/GWTBook/Samples/build/WEB-INF
/classes
    [copy] Copying 16 files to /home/pchaganti/dev/gwt-examples/GWTBook/Samples/build/WEB-INF/
lib
    [jar] Building jar: /home/pchaganti/dev/gwt-examples/GWTBook/Samples/build/WEB-INF/lib/gw
t-user-deploy.jar
    [zip] Building zip: /home/pchaganti/dev/gwt-examples/GWTBook/Samples/Samples.war

deploy-war:
    [copy] Copying 1 file to /home/pchaganti/dev/apache-tomcat-5.5.20/webapps

BUILD SUCCESSFUL
Total time: 2 minutes 39 seconds
pchaganti@pchaganti:~/dev/gwt-examples/GWTBook/Samples$
```

What Just Happened?

Apache Ant provides a great way to automate deploying our application. We create targets for cleaning out the old build artifacts, creating a WAR file, and deploying this WAR file to the Tomcat webapps directory. The applicationCreator command has an option for generating a simple build.xml file. We used this option to generate a skeleton build.xml file for our Samples project in Chapter 3. We took this generated file and modified it to add all the additional targets that we needed. We also packaged all the class files for our application into Samples.jar instead of copying the classes themselves.

Deployment from Eclipse

In the previous section, we created the build file that is used along with Ant to automate deployment of our application to Tomcat. However, we were running Ant from the command line. In this section, we will go through the steps needed to run Ant from inside Eclipse.

Time for Action—Running Ant from Eclipse

Here are the steps for running our build file from inside Eclipse:

1. Right-click the `Samples.ant.xml` file in the **Navigator** view in Eclipse. This will display the option for running Ant. Select **Run As | 1 Ant Build**:

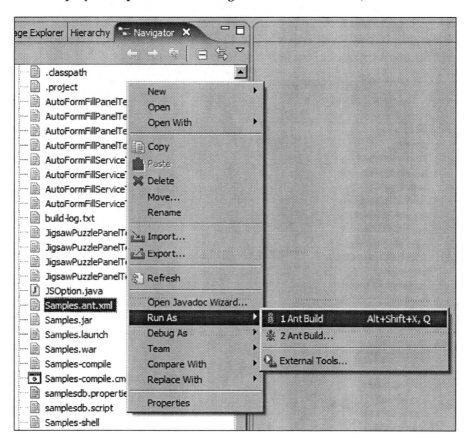

2. This will execute Ant and display the output by running the build in the **Console** view in Eclipse:

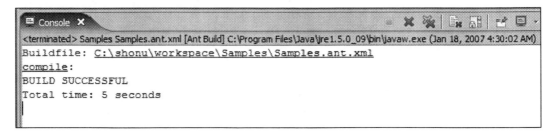

3. The previous screenshot shows the output of the `compile` target from the Ant script, which is the default target if you don't specify any other. Now we are going to run the `deploy-war` target. Right-click the `Samples.ant.xml` file again in the **Navigator** view in Eclipse. This time select **Run As | 2 Ant Build...** option, as shown in the following screenshot:

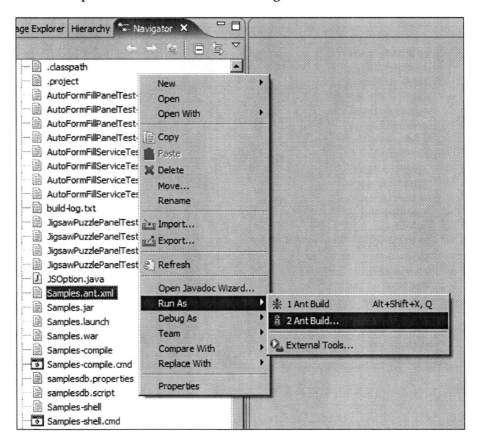

4. This will display the window where you can select which target to execute:

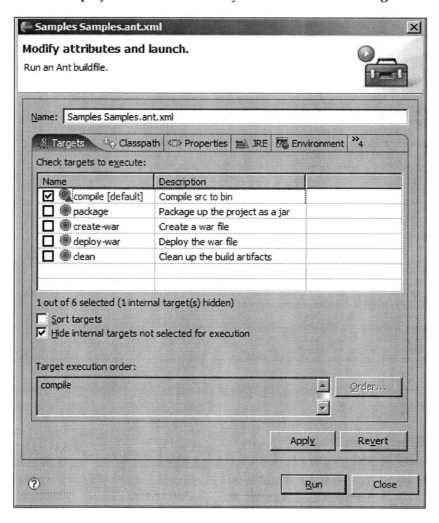

5. Select `deploy-war` and click **Run** to run the Ant build. The output will be displayed in the **Console** view in Eclipse:

```
Buildfile: C:\shonu\workspace\Samples\Samples.ant.xml
compile:
    [javac] Compiling 56 source files to C:\shonu\workspace\Samples\bin
    [javac] Note: Some input files use or override a deprecated API.
    [javac] Note: Recompile with -Xlint:deprecation for details.
clean:
    [delete] Deleting 143 files from C:\shonu\workspace\Samples\bin
    [delete] C:\shonu\workspace\Samples\www not found.
compile:
    [javac] Compiling 56 source files to C:\shonu\workspace\Samples\bin
    [javac] Note: Some input files use or override a deprecated API.
    [javac] Note: Recompile with -Xlint:deprecation for details.
package:
    [jar] Building jar: C:\shonu\workspace\Samples\Samples.jar
create-war:
    [copy] Copying 91 files to C:\shonu\workspace\Samples\build
   [mkdir] Created dir: C:\shonu\workspace\Samples\build\WEB-INF
    [copy] Copying 1 file to C:\shonu\workspace\Samples\build\WEB-INF
   [mkdir] Created dir: C:\shonu\workspace\Samples\build\WEB-INF\classes
    [copy] Copying 143 files to C:\shonu\workspace\Samples\build\WEB-INF\classes
   [mkdir] Created dir: C:\shonu\workspace\Samples\build\WEB-INF\lib
    [copy] Copying 6 files to C:\shonu\workspace\Samples\build\WEB-INF\lib
     [jar] Building jar: C:\shonu\workspace\Samples\build\WEB-INF\lib\gwt-user-deploy.jar
     [zip] Building zip: C:\shonu\workspace\Samples\Samples.war
deploy-war:
    [copy] Copying 1 file to C:\shonu\jakarta-tomcat-5.0.28\webapps
BUILD SUCCESSFUL
Total time: 3 minutes 52 seconds
```

Now we can run Ant from inside Eclipse and successfully deploy our application to Tomcat.

What Just Happened?

Eclipse provides excellent support for editing and running Ant build files. It recognizes `build.xml` files, and adds context actions to the various views so that you can right-click on a `build.xml` file and execute an Ant build. It also provides you with the option to run a specified target instead of just running the default target specified in the file. In this section, we learned how to use this support so that we can deploy to Tomcat directly from inside the Eclipse environment.

Summary

In this chapter, we learned to manually deploy our GWT application to Tomcat. Then, we saw how to automate the deployment with Ant, which lets us deploy our application from the command line.

Finally, we leveraged Eclipse's built-in Ant support to run our Ant build file from inside Eclipse.

Running the Samples

Here are the steps required to download and run the source code for the samples that we have developed in this book:

1. Download the ZIP file that contains the source code for our samples from the website for this book (http://www.packtpub.com/support). Unzip them to your hard disk. There should be two directories — Samples and Widgets — created when you unzip the file. These two directories contain the source code for the applications that we have developed in this book.

2. Start Eclipse 3.2. Create a new class path variable named GWT_HOME. Go to **Window | Preferences | Java | Build Path | Classpath Variables**. Add a new variable entry named GWT_HOME and set it to the directory where you have unzipped the GWT distribution, for example: C:\gwt-windows-1.3.1. This ensures that the GWT JAR files will be available to the samples project.

3. Import the two projects into your Eclipse workspace, one at a time. You can import an existing project into Eclipse by going to **File | Import | Existing projects into Workspace** and then selecting the root directory for the project. The Widgets project is used for creating the two widgets that are packaged up in a JAR file and used by the Samples project. It therefore does not define an entry point. All you need to do is run/debug the Samples project.

4. You can run the Samples project from inside Eclipse. Go to **Run | Run …** and select Samples. This will start up the familiar GWT shell and launch the hosted browser with the Samples application.

5. You can debug the Samples project from inside eclipse. Go to **Debug | Debug …** and select **Samples**.

6. If you have Apache Ant installed, you can use the `Samples.ant.xml` file to build the application and create a WAR file that can be used for deployment to a servlet container such as Tomcat.

7. You can also run the `Samples-compile.cmd` to compile the application and `Samples-shell.cmd` to run the application from a console on Windows.

Index

application, executing 30
application, generating 17, 25
application, modifying 22, 25
application, running in hosted mode 29
application, running in web mode 31
asynchronous service, testing 191
code, downloading 229
code, running 229
components 15, 16
downloading 8-10
files 11
forms 47
generating application, AJAX used 25
generating application, ApplicationCreator
        used 18-21
generating application, with Eclipse
        support 22
GWT hosted web browser, components 15
GWT Java-to-JavaScript compiler,
        components 15
interactive forms 47
interfaces 97
internationalization 201
internationalization, I18N support used
        201-205
JRE emulation library, components 16
JRE web UI class library, components 16
JUnit 187
KitchenSink 12-14
libraries 11
license 16
options, customizing 12
page, testing 187
page with asynchronous service, testing
        194, 195
sample code 229
samples, exploring 120-15
scripts 11
services, creating 35
test suite, creating 197
test suite, deploying 197
test suite, running 197
unit testing 187
user interfaces 97
widgets 153
XML, parsing on client 213-215

XML document, creating 208-211
XML support 207
GWT page
    testing 188, 189
    with asynchronous service, testing 194-196

I

interactive forms
    auto form fill 62
    dynamic lists 79
    edible labels, Flickr style 89
    live search 48
    password strength checker 55
    sample aaplication 47
    sortable tables 71
interfaces. *See* **user interfaces**
internationalization, GWT
    dynamic string internationalization 206
    I18N support, using 201-205
    static string internationalization 206
    techniques 205
    working 206

J

javascript library
    Moo.fx 128
    Rico color selector 140
    Rico rounded corners 136
    Scrip.aculo.us 145
Javascript Native Interface. *See* **JNSI**
JavaScript widgets 165
Java widgets 165
jigsaw puzzle
    about 120
    creating 120-124
JSNI
    about 127
    Moo.fx 128
    Rico color selector 140
    Rico rounded corners 136
    Scrip.aculo.us 145
    uses 127
JUnit 187

X

XML support, GWT

Packt Open Source Project Royalties

When we sell a book written on an Open Source project, we pay a royalty directly to that project. Therefore by purchasing Google Web Toolkit, Packt will have given some of the money received to the GWT project.

In the long term, we see ourselves and you—customers and readers of our books—as part of the Open Source ecosystem, providing sustainable revenue for the projects we publish on. Our aim at Packt is to establish publishing royalties as an essential part of the service and support a business model that sustains Open Source.

If you're working with an Open Source project that you would like us to publish on, and subsequently pay royalties to, please get in touch with us.

Writing for Packt

We welcome all inquiries from people who are interested in authoring. Book proposals should be sent to authors@packtpub.com. If your book idea is still at an early stage and you would like to discuss it first before writing a formal book proposal, contact us; one of our commissioning editors will get in touch with you.

We're not just looking for published authors; if you have strong technical skills but no writing experience, our experienced editors can help you develop a writing career, or simply get some additional reward for your expertise.

About Packt Publishing

Packt, pronounced 'packed', published its first book "Mastering phpMyAdmin for Effective MySQL Management" in April 2004 and subsequently continued to specialize in publishing highly focused books on specific technologies and solutions.

Our books and publications share the experiences of your fellow IT professionals in adapting and customizing today's systems, applications, and frameworks. Our solution-based books give you the knowledge and power to customize the software and technologies you're using to get the job done. Packt books are more specific and less general than the IT books you have seen in the past. Our unique business model allows us to bring you more focused information, giving you more of what you need to know, and less of what you don't.

Packt is a modern, yet unique publishing company, which focuses on producing quality, cutting-edge books for communities of developers, administrators, and newbies alike. For more information, please visit our website: www.PacktPub.com.

Printed in the United States
73335LV00004BA/143-152

9 781847 191007